More
ORIGAMI
for Children

More ORIGAMI *for Children*

35 FUN PAPER PROJECTS TO FOLD IN AN INSTANT

MARI ONO

CICO BOOKS
LONDON NEW YORK

Published in 2015 by CICO Books
An imprint of Ryland Peters & Small Ltd
20–21 Jockey's Fields   341 E 116th St
London WC1R 4BW   New York, NY 10029

www.rylandpeters.com

10 9 8 7 6 5 4 3 2 1

Text © Mari Ono 2015
Design and photography © CICO Books 2015

A CIP catalog record for this book is available from the
Library of Congress and the British Library.

ISBN: 978 1 78249 244 3

Printed in China

Editor: Robin Gurdon
Designer: Jerry Goldie
Step photography: Geoff Dann
Style photography: Terry Benson and Emma Mitchell
Stylist: Rob Merrett

Contents

Introduction

Origami, the art of folding paper, has long been a traditional activity for Japanese children. The skills required to make amazing origami models are passed from generation to generation. As the secrets of paper folding are shared, these skills evolve to create exciting new forms of origami, which then become part of this ancient art form that continues to develop.

In my previous book, *Origami for Children*, we looked into the traditional ways of folding origami. For this book I thought it would be fun to explore the modern style of folding origami.

To the casual observer, origami might sometimes seem like easy work—
simple folds repeatedly used to create a paper shape. However this view is
not always right. Origami does not necessarily start with shapes that will be
the same as those you can see in the finished model. In fact, the end result
is a collection of folds that are joined together to create something that's
unique to look at.

At first glance, some models might look a little complicated. Don't worry;
the steps are very easy to follow thanks to clear photography and step-by-
step instructions. Just give them a try, you'll be really surprised at what you
will be able to achieve. The beautiful thing about origami is its simplicity,
which means both adults and children can have fun mastering all the
essential techniques, helping them create countless beautiful origami models.

With *More Origami for Children* not only will a child's creative side be
encouraged, but it's also a great way for parents to play and have fun with
their kids. It is an astonishing moment when a piece of paper is transformed
into an origami model. Not only will everyone involved feel a sense of
accomplishment, but it also helps people to understand the concept of
simple beauty, which is a sense of fun and excitement that cannot be
obtained from games or watching TV. Most importantly, origami is a source
of creativity, and a source that's not just for the individual, but for a team...
your origami family!

INTRODUCTION

BASIC TECHNIQUES

The most basic skill of origami is folding paper precisely and creating strong, straight creases. This can be achieved through ensuring folded edges and corners match perfectly before firming up creases. To build up models more complicated folds are needed. Two of these are also explained here.

MAKING A FOLD

In origami the simplest fold is the most important so always take care to ensure every crease is perfectly straight.

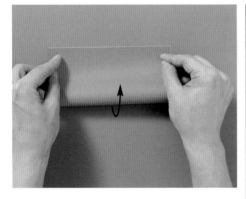

1 Always start by lining up the corners of the paper with each other to make sure they sit on top of each other.

2 Holding the turned paper in place with one hand carefully press down both ends of the new fold.

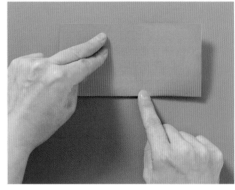

3 Only when you are sure the folded paper is perfectly in position should you press down the length of the fold.

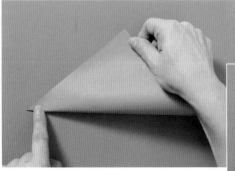

4 Fold from corner to corner in the same way, first ensuring that the edges of the paper are aligned with one another.

5 Always keep one hand on the paper during the fold and only release once the crease has been firmly pressed into place.

MAKING A TRIANGLE FOLD

This technique converts a square shape into a triangle that can then be used as the basis for any number of origami models.

1 Fold the paper from top to bottom then fold it in half again making a square.

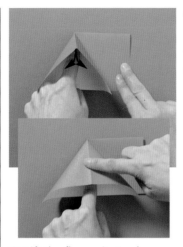

2 Lift the flap so it stands straight up and then open it up by pressing the fold down toward you into a triangle shape.

3 Press the new diagonal edges flat, making firm creases.

MAKING AN OUTSIDE FOLD

This technique is used to enclose the majority of a sheet inside one folded corner.

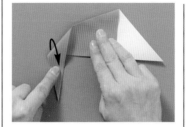

1 Start with a folded model, usually with the creased edge toward you, and turn over one end at an angle, making a firm crease.

2 Open out the sheet and begin to fold the tip down, reversing the direction of one of the diagonal creases and the central crease as you go.

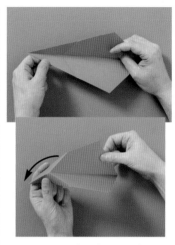

3 When the sheet is flattened the folded corner will be surrounding the main body of the paper at a distinct angle.

KEY TO ARROWS

FOLD
Fold the part of the paper shown in this direction.

FOLDING DIRECTION
Fold the entire paper over in this direction.

OPEN OUT
Open out and refold the paper over in the direction shown.

CHANGE THE POSITION
Spin the paper 90° in the direction of the arrows.

TURN OVER
Turn the paper over.

CHANGE THE POSITION
Spin the paper through 180°.

MAKE A CREASE
Fold the paper over in the direction of the arrow then open it out again.

CHAPTER ONE

Cute Critters and Pretty Flowers

1 ELEPHANT

Difficulty rating: ● ○ ○

The elephant is the biggest and most magnificent animal in the world but this origami model shows his gentle and playful side. It is also very simple to make so is the perfect introduction to the art of origami. Remember to make the folds crisp and completely even.

You will need:
One sheet of 6 in (15 cm) square paper

1 With the design side down, fold the paper in half through the design to make a crease then fold in both of the right-hand edges so that they meet along the central crease.

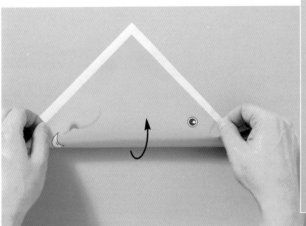

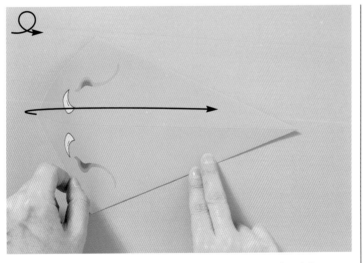

2 Turn the paper over, keeping the narrow point on the right, then fold the left point over so that it sits on top of the right-hand point.

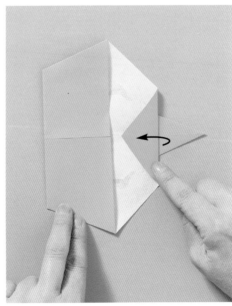

3 Fold back the right-hand point of the top sheet so that it touches the vertical edge of the colored paper.

CUTE CRITTERS AND PRETTY FLOWERS

4 Fold in the top and bottom points to make short horizontal edges then turn over the corners on the left-hand side in the same way.

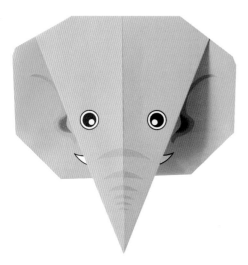

2 CAT

Where would we be without the gentle playful pussy cat to look after us? As well as being fun she is also very wise, even when she is starting to grow old. Make this charming model using two pieces of paper and use paper glue to make sure they are firmly stuck together.

You will need:
Two sheets of 6 in (15 cm) square paper
Paper glue

1 Take the sheet with the face design side down and fold it from corner to corner through the design to make a crease. Open the paper up and fold the top down to the bottom to make a fold across the design.

2 Fold the outer points down to the bottom so that the top edges meet along the central crease then turn over the new top point using the marks on the paper as a guide.

CUTE CRITTERS AND PRETTY FLOWERS

3 Turn up the two flaps made in the last step, using the marks on the paper as a guide, then fold up the bottom point to make a horizontal edge.

4 Take the second sheet design side down and fold it from corner to corner through the design to make a crease. Open the paper up and fold the bottom point up to the top, making a fold across the design, then fold up the right-hand point so that the bottom edge now runs along the central crease.

4 Fold up the bottom point to make a horizontal base then turn the paper over and fold in the edges to give the tree trunk straight edges.

5 BUTTERFLY

Butterflies dancing through the air are one of the most beautiful sights of summer. Recreate that vision with this amazingly simple yet vivid origami model. Use the paper supplied here then make up your own designs to create a whole cloud of colorful butterflies.

Difficulty rating: ● ○ ○

You will need:
One sheet of 6 in (15 cm) square paper

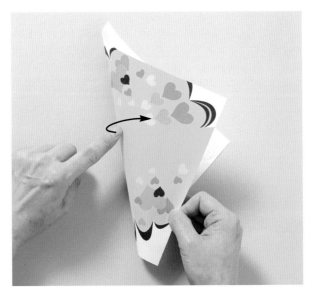

1 With the design side down, fold over the left-hand side at a slight angle using the line marked on the paper as a guide, ensuring that the corners do not align.

2 Fold up the bottom of the paper using the line marked on the design to form the insect's wings and press flat.

CUTE CRITTERS AND PRETTY FLOWERS

6 RABBIT

The cheeky rabbit hops out of his burrow to nibble at the flowers and
vegetables in the garden. He might be naughty but is always happy.
This model uses an outside fold to make the rabbit's head so check the
Techniques section at the beginning of the book if you have any trouble.

You will need:
One sheet of 6 in (15 cm) square paper

1 With the design side down, fold the paper in half from corner to corner through the design to make a crease then open it out and fold the left-hand edges in so that they meet along the center line. Fold the paper in half along the same crease.

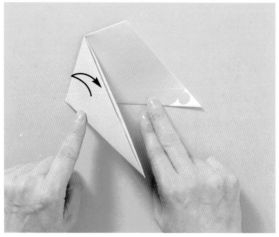

2 Fold down the left-hand point at an angle, using the lines marked on the paper as a guide, and make a sharp crease.

3 Open out the paper and turn it over. Carefully lift the left-hand point and begin to fold it back on itself, using the creases just made as the fold lines, though reversing the direction of the folds where necessary.

4 Continue to close up the model by pressing the two halves of the body together while flattening the long point which forms the rabbit's neck and head.

7 TULIP

When the tulips flower in the garden you can be sure that Spring has truly arrived, each growing straight up in the air with a beautiful colored bloom. This pretty pink flower could be one of many that you could make in every color of the rainbow—from the darkest blue to purest white.

You will need:
One sheet of 6 in (15 cm) square paper

1 With the design side down, fold in half from corner to corner through the design to make a crease then open again and fold the bottom point up to the top.

2 Fold up the bottom left corner using the line marked on the paper as a guide ensuring that the point breaks over the diagonal edge. Turn the paper over and repeat.

3 Fold in the right-hand point at a slight angle to make a crease then repeat on the left-hand side.

CUTE CRITTERS AND PRETTY FLOWERS

4 Open up the model and fold the side points inside, reversing the direction of the creases where necessary.

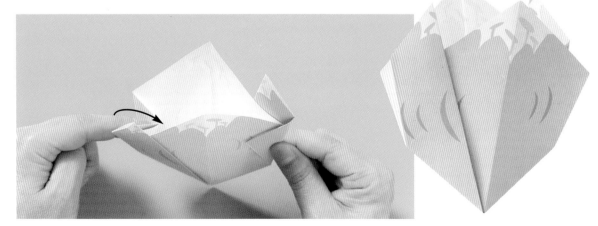

8 CHRYSANTHEMUM

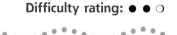
Chrysanthemums have long been highly valued in Japan for their large, round flowers, their delicacy, and the huge variety of colors and sizes. This origami model is made from three sheets of paper but each one must first be cut into four so you will end up folding 12 small sheets to make the model. Take care not to use too much paper glue or you might spoil the beautiful design.

You will need:
Three sheets of 15 cm (6 in) square paper
Scissors
Paper glue

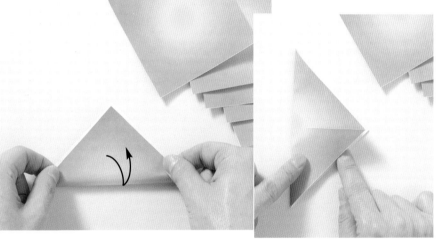

1 First cut the three sheets of paper along the lines marked on the sheets to make 12 smaller squares. Put the four squares for the leaf to one side.

2 With the design side of a flower square down, fold the bottom point up to the top, make a firm crease then open out again before folding the left-hand point over to the right.

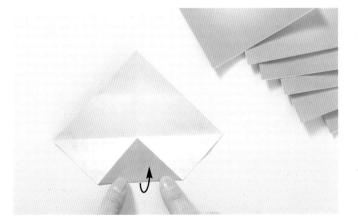

3 Open the paper out again and fold the bottom point up to the central crease.

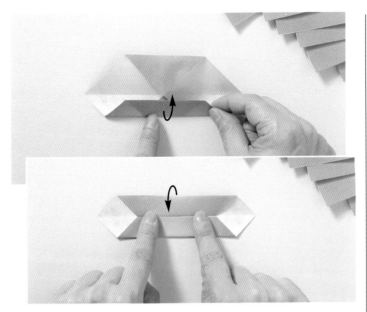

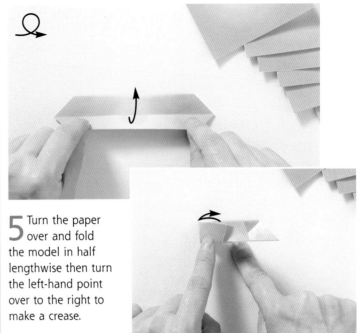

4 Fold down the top point in the same way then fold up the bottom edge to the central crease. Again repeat at the top.

5 Turn the paper over and fold the model in half lengthwise then turn the left-hand point over to the right to make a crease.

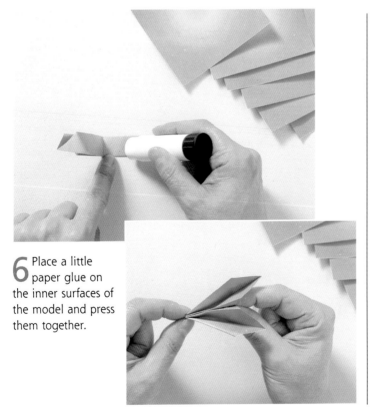

6 Place a little paper glue on the inner surfaces of the model and press them together.

7 Repeat the whole process with the seven other sheets that make up the flower then use paper glue to stick them together to form the circular bloom.

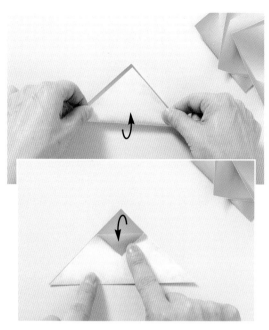

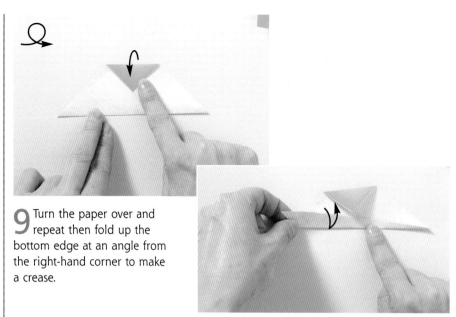

9 Turn the paper over and repeat then fold up the bottom edge at an angle from the right-hand corner to make a crease.

8 Take the first sheet for the leaf design side up and fold it in half from corner to corner across the paper, then turn down the tip of the upper sheet halfway toward the bottom edge.

11 Turn the model over and fold over the bottom corners of the colored triangles to soften the shape of the leaf.

10 Open out the fold you just made then turn down the upper sheet of the model, using the crease line as your fold line.

9 WHALE

The huge but gentle whale glides effortlessly through the sea, breaking the surface to breathe before diving into the dark and hidden depths of the ocean—who knows where it will reappear? This model also uses two pieces of paper stuck together. Take care to use as little glue as possible so that the sheets remain easy to fold.

Difficulty rating: ● ○ ○

You will need:
Two sheets of 6 in (15 cm)
square paper
Paper glue

1 Take the two sheets and stick them together, with the patterns as shown, by placing a little paper glue in the corners and along the edges. Press together and wait for the glue to dry.

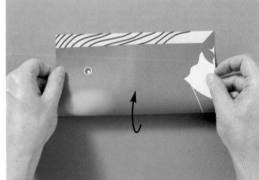

2 Fold the bottom edge up so that it sits approximately ½ in (1 cm) below the top edge and make a crease.

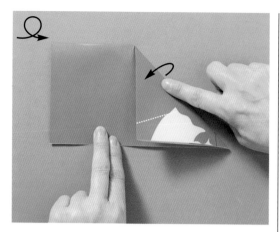

3 Turn the paper over so that the crease is at the top and fold down the top right corner at an angle so that it sits on the bottom edge.

4 Turn over the bottom right corner at an angle, using the line marked on the paper as a guide, then fold back both left-hand corners as shown.

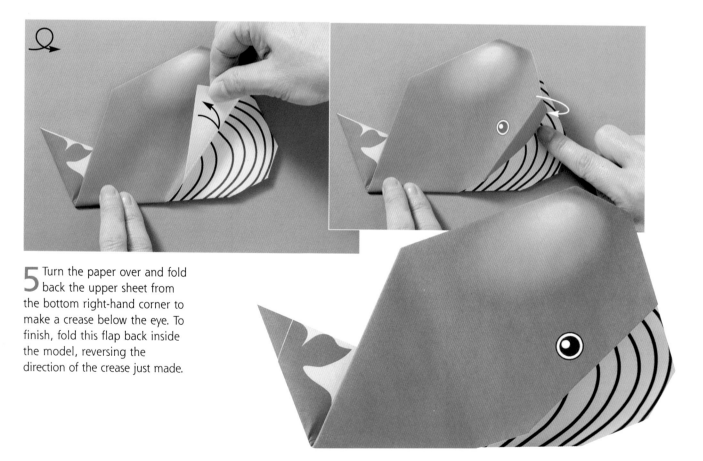

5 Turn the paper over and fold back the upper sheet from the bottom right-hand corner to make a crease below the eye. To finish, fold this flap back inside the model, reversing the direction of the crease just made.

10 PARAKEET

Difficulty rating: ● ● ○

You will need:
One sheet of 15 cm (6 in) square paper

These beautifully colored, small parrots zoom around the forest sky squawking and shrieking as they dash from tree to tree. Some are green, some blue, and others a mixture of the two but all are as fast and lively as can be imagined. Take care when folding the wings on this origami model as you want to be sure to make them as even as you can.

1 With the design side down, fold the bottom point up to the top, make a firm crease then open out again before folding the left-hand point over to the right.

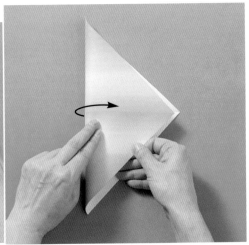

2 Now fold the right-hand point back across the paper to the left, ensuring that the line of the head in the design runs down the right edge of the paper.

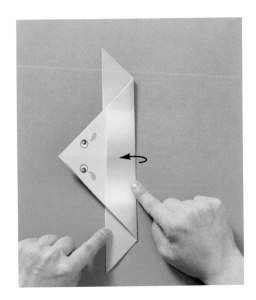

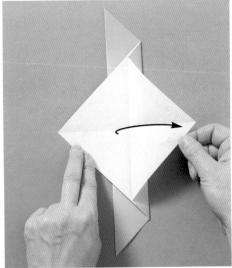

3 Fold back the upper sheet of the left-hand point to form a diamond, making the crease in the middle of the paper on the bottom layer.

34

CUTE CRITTERS AND PRETTY FLOWERS

4 Fold the object in half by bringing the top point down to the bottom then fold up the top layer of paper from the bottom point at a slight angle to form the wing, making the crease across the bird's body.

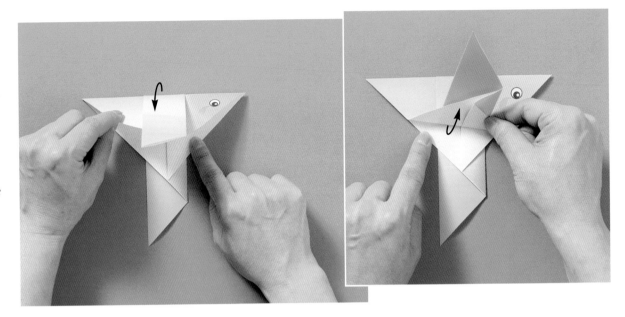

5 Turn the model over and repeat with the other wing.

6 Turn over the beak at an angle to make a crease then open up the head slightly and refold the beak inside, reversing the direction of the creases where necessary.

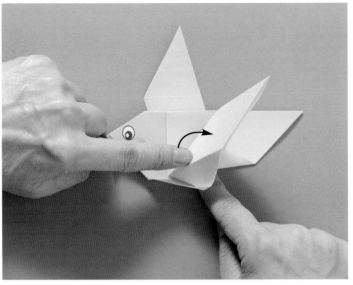

7 Start making the bend in the wing by gently inserting a finger underneath the flap at the base of the wing and pulling it open.

8 As the flap opens the wing turns back and the base opens out, creating a new fold at an angle across the wing.

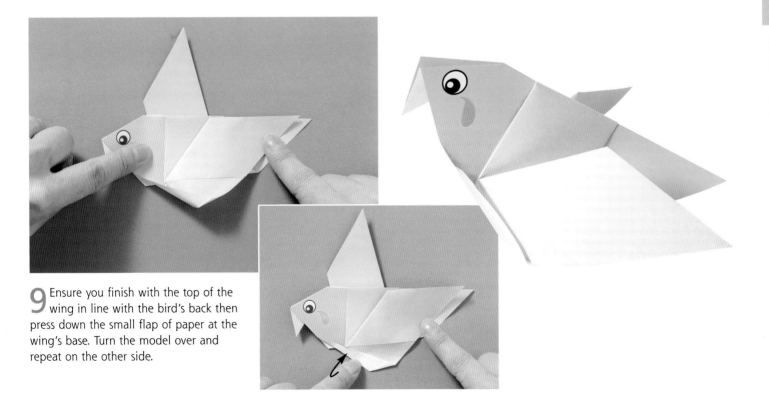

9 Ensure you finish with the top of the wing in line with the bird's back then press down the small flap of paper at the wing's base. Turn the model over and repeat on the other side.

11 SQUIRREL

Scampering about among the falling leaves, the squirrel searches for nuts to hide away in preparation for the long winter ahead. Racing up and down tree trunks, jumping from branch to branch, he never seems to stop for a moment. Take special care to align all the folds exactly so that the two parts of the animal sit together perfectly.

You will need:
Two sheets of 6 in (15 cm) square paper
Paper glue

1 With the design side down, fold the paper in half from corner to corner through the design to make a crease then open out and make a fold across the design. Turn over the top point using the lines marked on the paper as a guide.

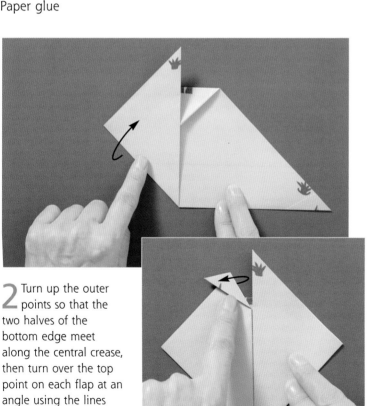

2 Turn up the outer points so that the two halves of the bottom edge meet along the central crease, then turn over the top point on each flap at an angle using the lines marked on the paper.

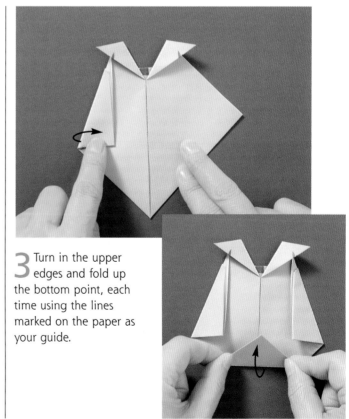

3 Turn in the upper edges and fold up the bottom point, each time using the lines marked on the paper as your guide.

CUTE CRITTERS AND PRETTY FLOWERS

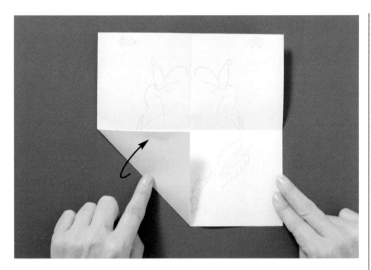

4 Take the second sheet and with the design side down fold it in half both ways, opening it out each time to make creases then fold in the bottom corners so that they meet at the center point.

5 Fold over the diagonal edges so that they meet along the vertical crease, making two new diagonal edges.

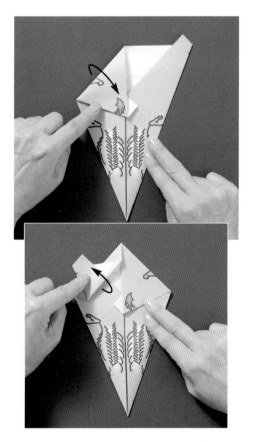

6 Fold down the top two corners so that the two halves of the upper edge now meet along the middle of the model. Fold back the corners across the new diagonal folds, using the lines marked on the paper as a guide.

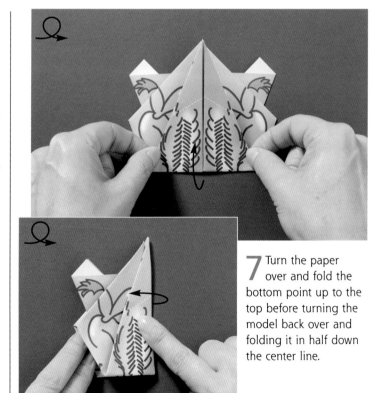

7 Turn the paper over and fold the bottom point up to the top before turning the model back over and folding it in half down the center line.

8 Lift the model off the table and gently pull the outer flap away from the body to form the tail. Lay it back on the table and press flat the new creases, before turning over the tip at an angle to make a crease as shown.

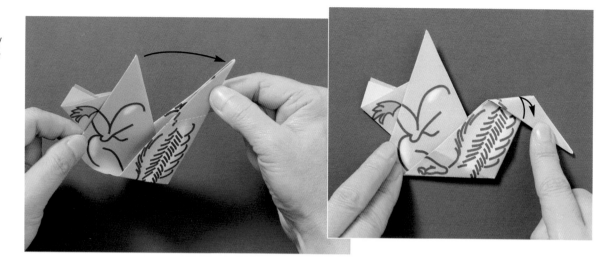

9 Lifting the model off the table open out the flap and fold the tip back around the rest of the paper, reversing the direction of the folds where necessary.

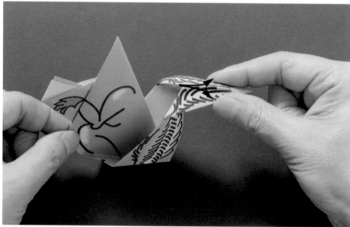

10 Cover the top of the body with paper glue and position the head against it, pressing the two pieces together.

CHAPTER TWO
Sweet Treats

12 GRAPES

The rich, glossy grapes are packed with juice and goodness, full of delicious flavor. Each bunch is made up of 12 individual grapes so check they are as even as possible before sticking them onto the branch. Remember to place them in front or behind each other randomly, just like a real bunch of grapes.

You will need:
Two sheets of 6 in (15 cm) square paper
Scissors
Paper glue

1 Cut up both sheets of paper along the lines marked. You will have enough pieces to make 12 grapes and two stalks.

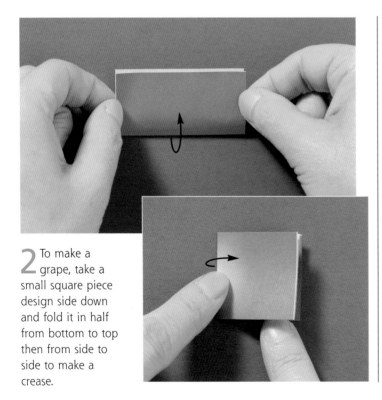

2 To make a grape, take a small square piece design side down and fold it in half from bottom to top then from side to side to make a crease.

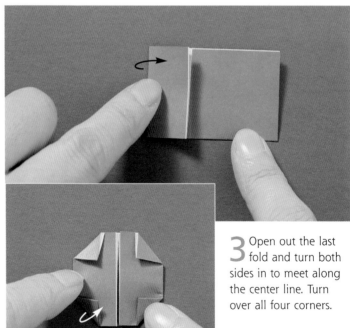

3 Open out the last fold and turn both sides in to meet along the center line. Turn over all four corners.

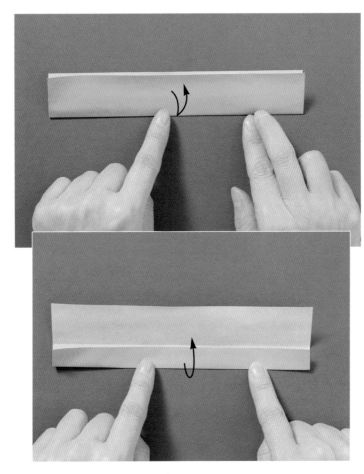

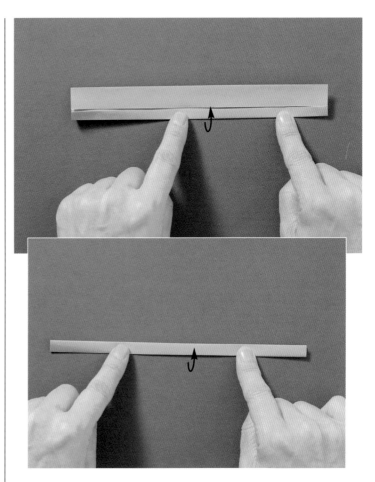

4 Now take the long piece design side down and fold it in half lengthwise to make a crease. Open it up again and fold the top and bottom edges in to meet along the center line.

5 Fold the top and bottom edges in again to meet in the center before folding the piece in half.

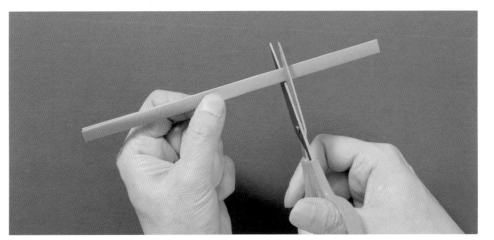

6 Cut one end off about a third of the way along.

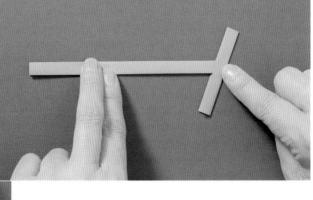

7 Open out the long piece and, using paper glue, stick the two sides back together. Repeat on the short piece then stick it across one end of the long piece of paper.

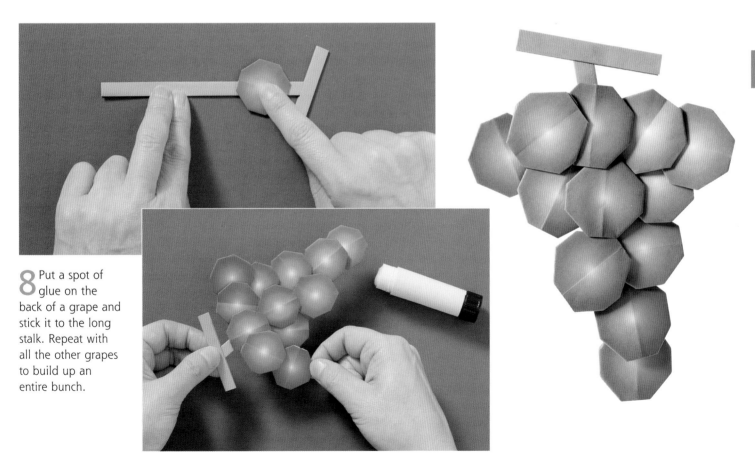

8 Put a spot of glue on the back of a grape and stick it to the long stalk. Repeat with all the other grapes to build up an entire bunch.

13 DOUGHNUT

A doughnut is a treat that you know is slightly naughty but is so delicious you can't stop yourself from enjoying. This one is a ring covered in icing and colored stars and sprinkles—just perfect to make you feel better in the middle of the day. What's even better is that is so easy to make.

You will need:
One sheet of 6 in (15 cm) square paper

1 With the design side down, fold the paper in half from corner to corner both ways to make creases, opening out each time, then fold the corners in so that they meet at the center point.

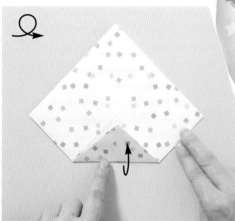

2 Turn the paper over and fold the corners in again. Fold in the new corners halfway toward the center point.

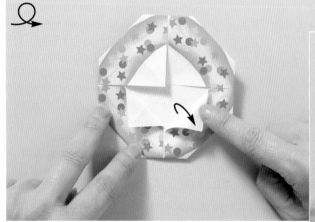

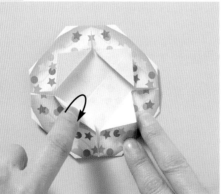

3 Turn the paper over and fold the points back from the center, ensuring you don't crease through any of the design, then tuck the tips inside and underneath, reversing the direction of the creases just made.

SWEET TREATS

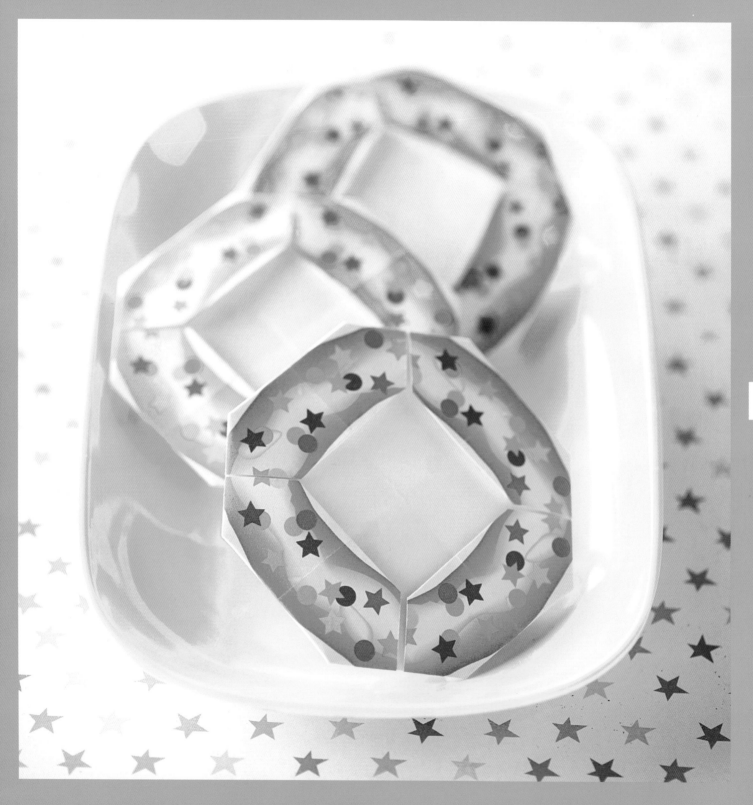

14 CANDY

Unwrapping a sugar candy is a pleasure that few can resist. Making a bowlful of these little origami sweets might be a good way of stopping yourself eating too many of the real thing! The ends of each model can be made slightly differently to replicate the different sweets.

Difficulty rating: ● ● ○

You will need:
One sheet of 6 in (15 cm) square paper

1 With the design side down, fold the paper in half both ways to make creases, opening out each time, then fold the corners in so that they meet at the center point. Next fold the top and bottom points in to meet at the center point.

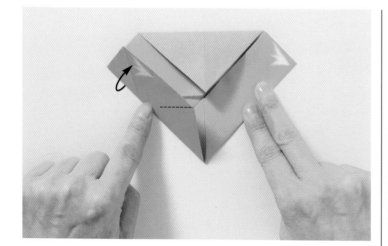

2 Fold the lower diagonal edges over so that they align along the edges of the upper triangle made in the previous step.

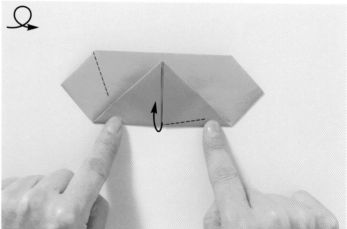

3 Turn the paper over and fold up the bottom triangle so that the tip touches the top edge.

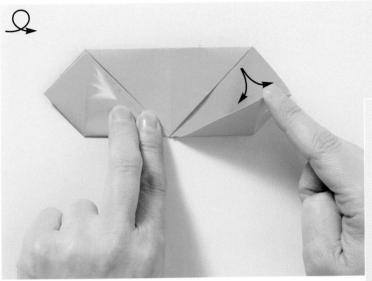

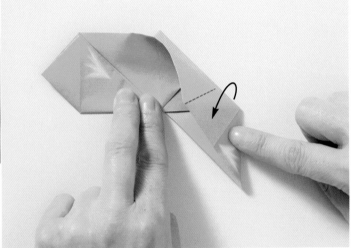

4 Turn the paper back over and pull forward the tip of the right-hand flap so that the outer edge folds over and the top edge runs down the center line.

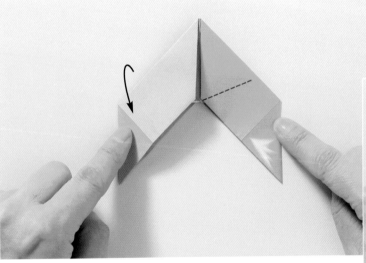

5 Repeat on the left-hand flap then turn the top flap down.

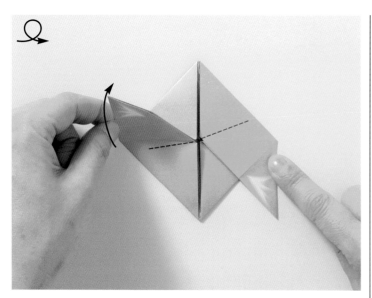

6 Turn the paper over and fold up the left-hand flap.

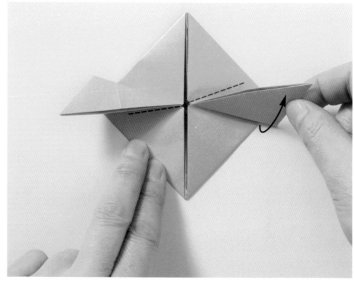

7 Fold over both flaps so that the edges run along the lines marked at angles on the paper.

8 Finish by folding in the top and bottom points so that they meet at the center of the model.

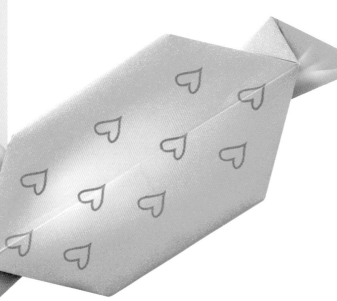

15 STRAWBERRY CAKE

How much simpler to make an origami model of a strawberry cake than bake one! It may not taste quite as good as the real thing but will still give you the feeling of a tea party on a sunny summer afternoon. Check the lines marked on the paper as they will help you make all your folds in the right place.

You will need:
One sheet of 6 in (15 cm) square paper

1 With the design side up, fold the paper in half both ways to make creases, opening out each time.

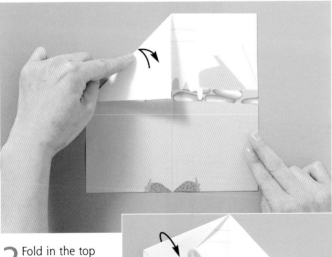

2 Fold in the top corners to meet at the center point, making creases, then open them out again and fold the edges in to run along the creases just made.

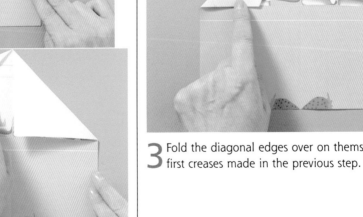

3 Fold the diagonal edges over on themselves using the first creases made in the previous step.

SWEET TREATS

4 Fold over the top tip so that it sits in line with the edges of the flaps just made to make a crease. Open it out and fold over the point again, this time halfway to the crease just made.

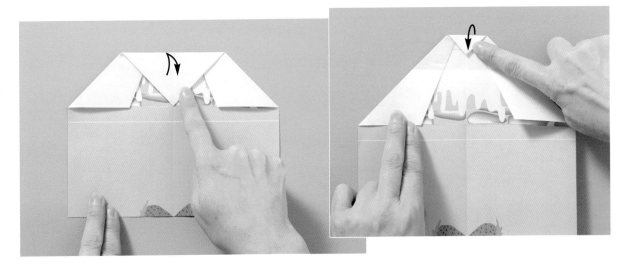

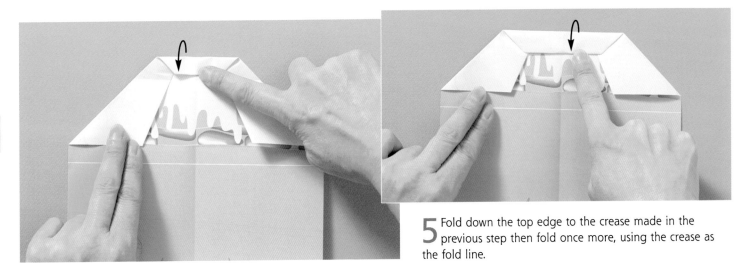

5 Fold down the top edge to the crease made in the previous step then fold once more, using the crease as the fold line.

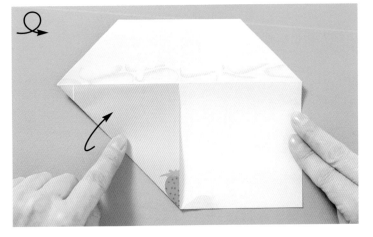

6 Turn the paper over and fold up the bottom points so that they meet on the crease lines.

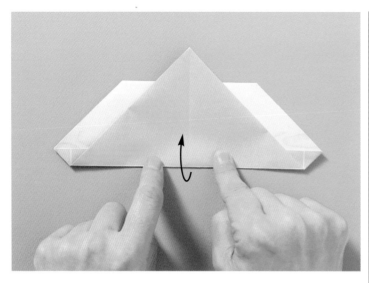

7 Fold up the bottom point using the lines marked on the paper as a guide.

8 Fold in the side points to make creases, ensuring they meet in the center, then open them out again and refold the points to the creases just made.

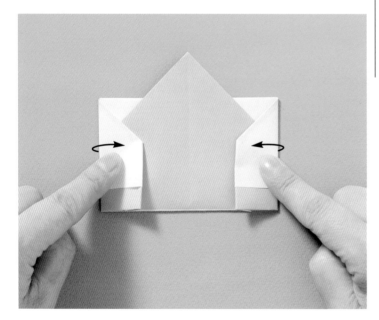

9 Finish by refolding the creases made in the previous step.

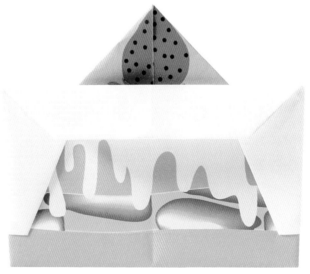

16 ICE CREAM

Eating an ice cream in a cone is the perfect way to round off a day in the park, on the beach, or at a country fair. If you would like to enjoy one without the pure white of the frozen cream dripping over the edge of the biscuit cone why not try making this origami model?

Difficulty rating: ● ○ ○

You will need:
One sheet of 6 in (15 cm)
square paper

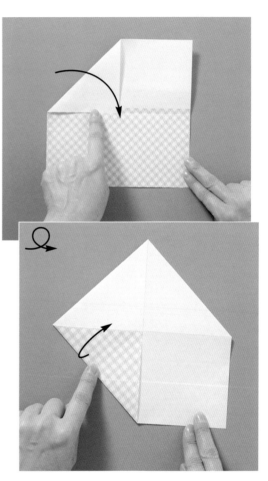

1 With the design side up, fold the paper in half both ways to make creases, opening out each time, then fold the top two corners to the center. Turn the paper over and fold up the bottom two corners to the center.

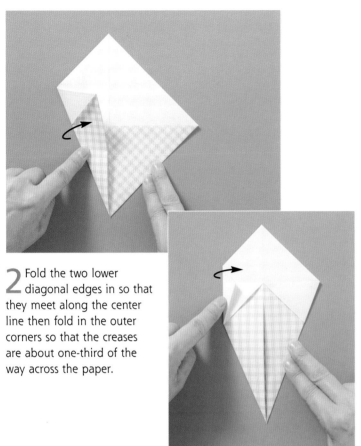

2 Fold the two lower diagonal edges in so that they meet along the center line then fold in the outer corners so that the creases are about one-third of the way across the paper.

3 Fold down the top point, making the crease line across the top of the existing flaps, then turn back the tip to make a concertina fold.

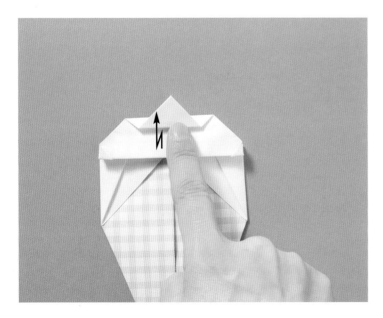

4 Finish by making a second concertina fold nearer the tip.

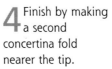

17 CUPCAKE

Every afternoon tea should involve a plate of cupcakes, the best—like this one—with a cherry on top and covered in sprinkles. As you make the origami model take care to fold the edges at the correct angles so that the sides are even and the cupcakes stay completely symmetrical.

Difficulty rating: ● ● ○

You will need:
One sheet of 6 in (15 cm) square paper

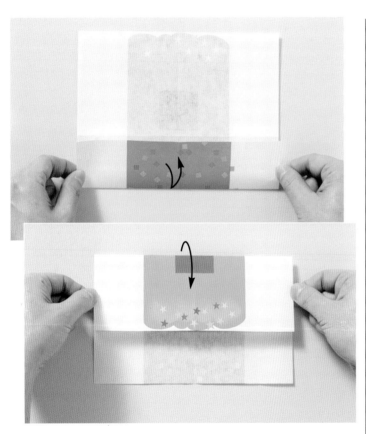

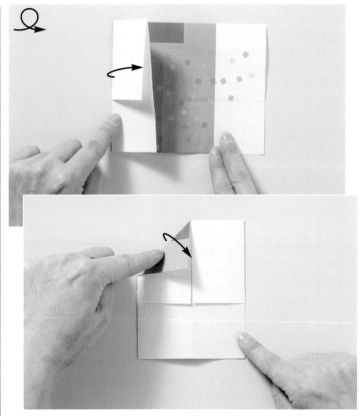

1 With the design side down, fold the paper in half both ways to make creases, opening out each time, then fold up the bottom edge to the horizontal crease and open again. Turn down the top edge to the lower crease.

2 Turn the paper over and fold the sides in so that they meet in the center, then turn down the top corners so that they also meet on the center line.

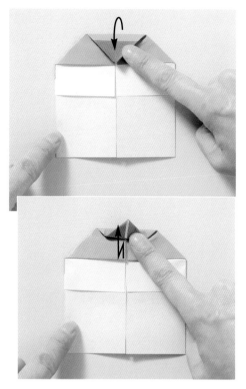

3 Fold the top point down to the colored edge then turn back the point to make a concertina fold.

4 Turn over the bottom corners at an angle so that they touch the center line, ensuring that the crease runs inside the flap above, then finish by folding up the bottom edge to the flap.

18 GIFT BOX

Place all your goodies in this colorful gift box—it's just perfect for holding all the origami candies, cupcakes, and doughnuts you have made— that's as strong and solid as you will ever need. Using the triangle fold will give the box a strong base so take care to ensure that all your creases are as even as possible.

You will need:
One sheet of rectangular paper

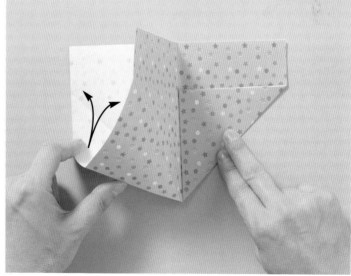

1 With the design side down fold the paper in half across its width then fold it in half again the other way to make a crease, and open out.

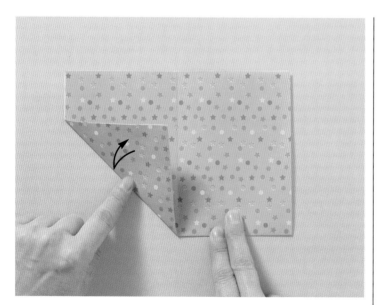

2 Fold the bottom corners up and across to meet on the center line to make diagonal creases.

3 Open out the crease made in the last step and lift the flap's top sheet. Begin to push the bottom corner up and inside the flap, reversing the direction of the front diagonal crease.

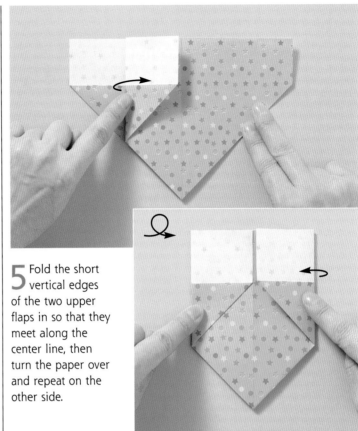

4 Push the corner all the way inside the flap so that what was the bottom edge now runs up the center line, then close the flap on top. Repeat on the other side.

5 Fold the short vertical edges of the two upper flaps in so that they meet along the center line, then turn the paper over and repeat on the other side.

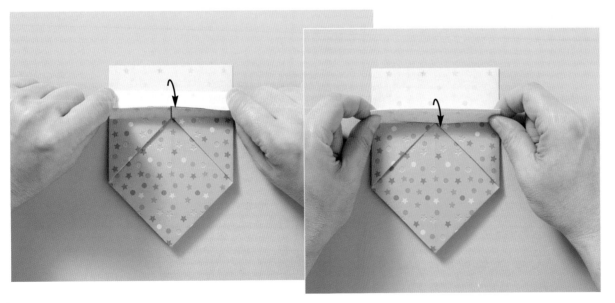

6 Fold the top edge of the front flap down to run along the horizontal edge of paper below, then fold this flap over again to cover that edge. Turn the paper over and repeat on the other side.

7 Fold up the bottom points to make a horizontal crease between the bottom points of the two vertical edges.

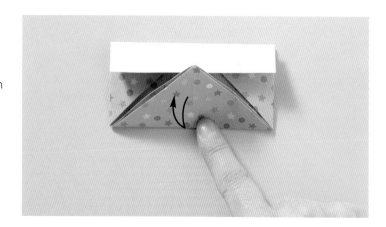

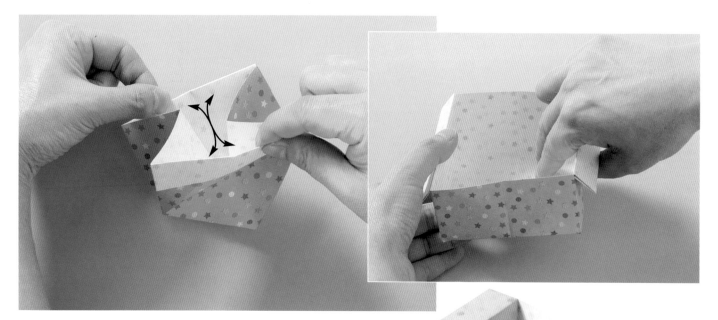

8 Lift up the paper and gently start to open up the model into a square. As you straighten the sides the box's flat base should form by itself.

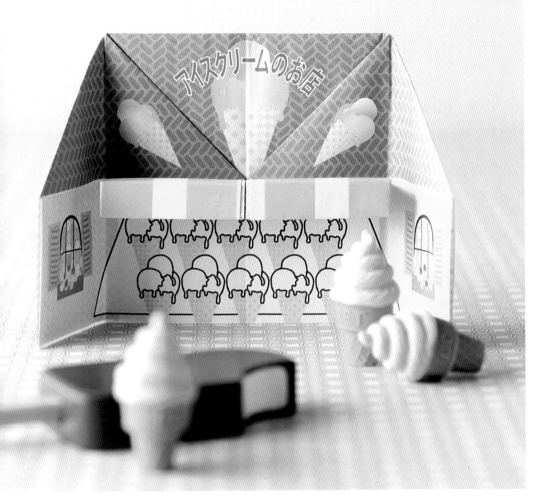

1 Take the two sheets and stick them together, with the patterns as shown, by placing a little paper glue in the corners and along the edges. Press together and wait for the glue to dry.

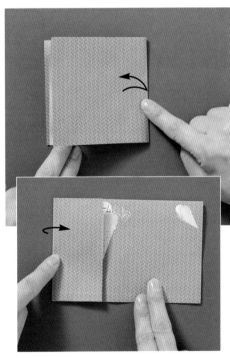

19 CANDY STORE

The best store in town is the one that sells all the candy, cakes, and ice creams anyone could desire. You can recreate it with this origami model that brings to life those sweet smells and delicious-tasting treats. Once again the creases are vital to give you a symmetrical model that will stand up with its awning shading all those goodies!

You will need:
Two sheets of 6 in (15 cm) square paper

Difficulty rating: ● ○ ○

2 Fold the paper in half from top to bottom. Fold again from side to side to make a crease. Open out and fold the two sides in so that they meet along the center line.

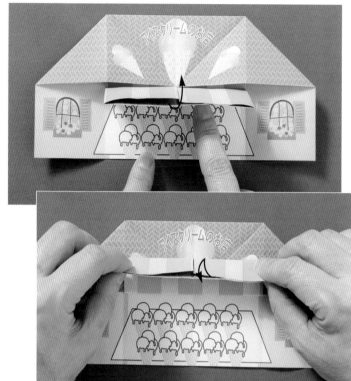

3 Make a triangle fold by opening up the flap made in the previous step and pressing the two halves flat to form a triangle at the top. Repeat on the other side.

4 Take the large flap in the center and fold it up, using the bases of the triangles as the fold line. Next fold down the top of this flap to make a crease.

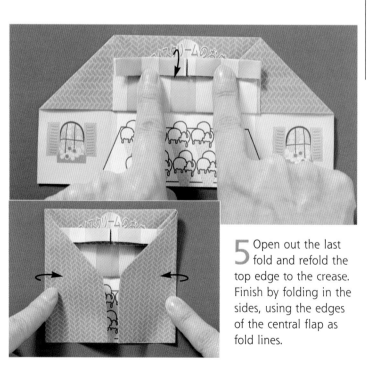

5 Open out the last fold and refold the top edge to the crease. Finish by folding in the sides, using the edges of the central flap as fold lines.

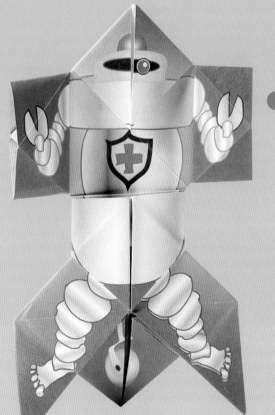

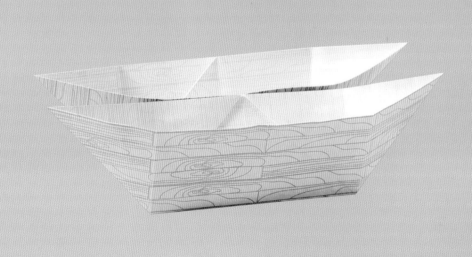

CHAPTER THREE

Play Time!

20 PUPPET

These friendly little finger puppets will make every playtime fun. First enjoy making them then have hours of fun acting out scenes with the happy animals. Remember to use the glue sparingly—just enough to hold the model together but not so much that the paper becomes too stiff.

Difficulty rating: ● ● ○

You will need:
One sheet of 6 in (15 cm) square paper
Paper glue

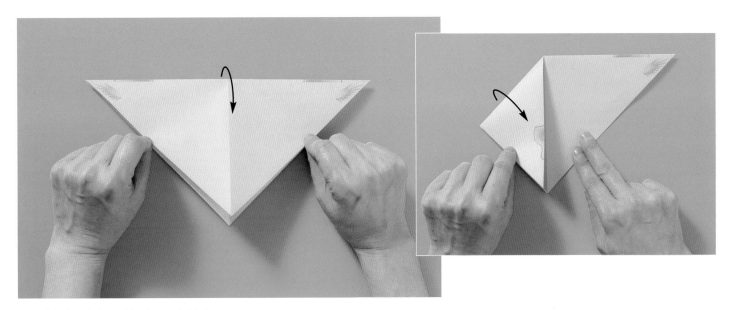

1 With the design side down, fold the paper in half from corner to corner through the design to make a crease. Open out then fold in half the other way before folding the outer corners down to the bottom point.

2 Fold up the flaps just made at an angle, creating the crease line from the outer corners to a point approximately one third of the way down the center line.

3 Fold up the bottom point, making a crease between the two outer points, and release.

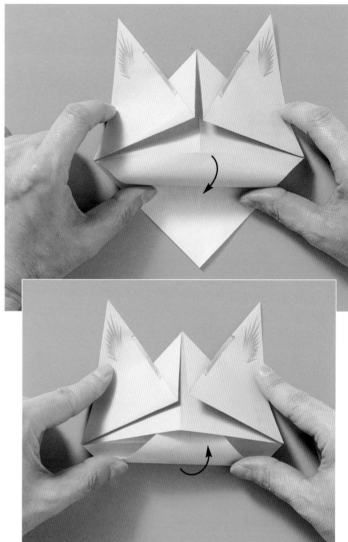

4 Fold the bottom point of the upper flap inside the model then repeat with the lower flap.

5 Fold in the outer points so that they meet on the center line.

6 Fold down the top point, making a horizontal fold between the model's ears.

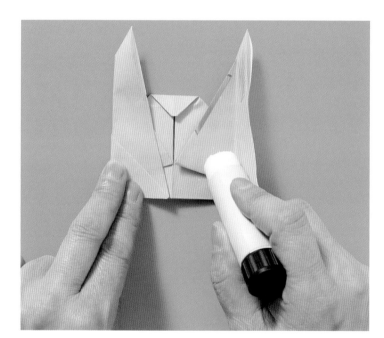

7 Stick down the two flaps made in step 5 using paper glue.

21 HORNED HELMET

The Japanese horned helmet was worn by warriors for centuries so your origami model will look good on any action figure from any age. The pattern on this sheet evokes the ancient art of Japan but you could use any pattern that might be in keeping with the model who will wear it.

You will need:
One sheet of 6 in (15 cm) square paper

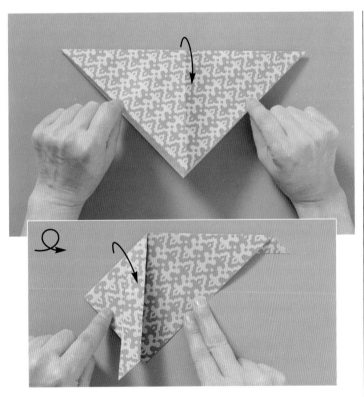

1 With the design side down, fold the paper in half from corner to corner to make a crease. Open out then fold in half the other way. Turn over the top edge by approximately ½ in (1 cm) before turning the paper over and folding the outer corners down to the bottom point.

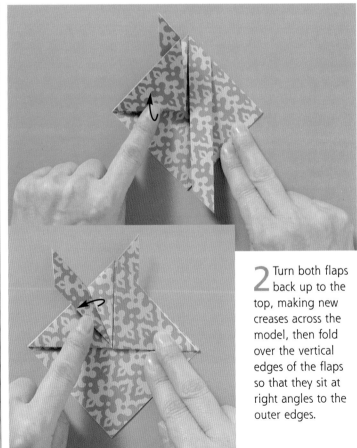

2 Turn both flaps back up to the top, making new creases across the model, then fold over the vertical edges of the flaps so that they sit at right angles to the outer edges.

PLAY TIME!

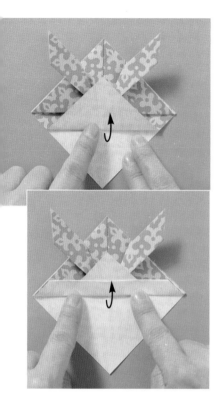

3 Turn up the upper flap from the bottom, making a crease about ½ in (1 cm) below the horizontal edge, then fold it over again using the bottom edges as the fold line.

4 Finish by folding the remaining bottom point up inside the model.

22 POINTED HELMET

Although similar in some respects to the horned helmet this pointed version is more appropriate for Japanese gentlemen rather than soldiers. Its tall shape is surprisingly easy to make so why not create a whole range to give your dolls and figures a different look for each day?

You will need:
One sheet of 6 in (15 cm) square paper

1 With the design side down, fold the paper in half from corner to corner to make a crease. Open out then fold in half the other way. Turn the two outer points down to the bottom then fold in the two upper edges so that they meet along the center line.

2 Fold up the bottom points over the edges of the flaps made in the last step then fold back the tips half way across themselves.

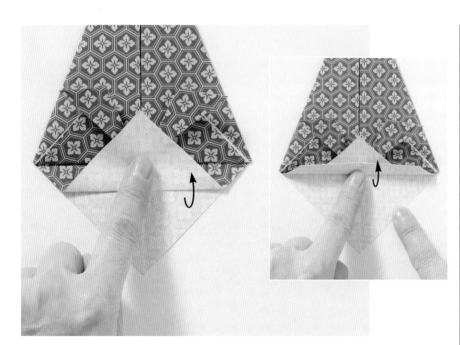

3 Turn up the upper flap from the bottom, making a crease about ½ in (1 cm) below the horizontal edge then fold it over again using the bottom edge as the fold line.

4 Finish by folding the remaining bottom point up inside the model.

23 CARD SUITS

Difficulty rating: ● ● ○

You will need:
Five sheets of 6 in (15 cm)
square paper
Scissors
Paper glue

Playing cards are popular all over the world and the four suits are recognizable wherever you find them. The diamonds are particularly simple and you could also use the heart as a token for someone special, but take care with the spades and clubs—they are tricky to make evenly and you also need to be careful when you glue the two parts together.

Diamonds

1 Cut a sheet of paper into quarters. Taking one small sheet design side down, fold it in half from corner to corner to make a crease before opening it out.

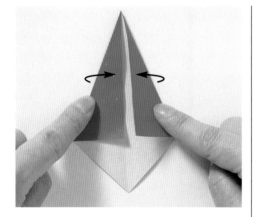

2 Fold the upper edges in to meet along the center line.

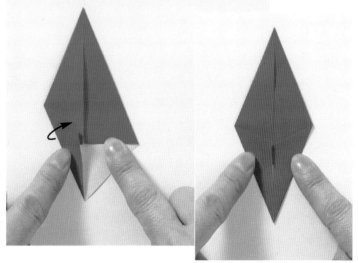

3 Fold both lower edges up to the center line in the same way to create the diamond shape.

Spades

1 Take the first sheet design side down and fold it in half from corner to corner both ways, opening out each time to make creases, then turn the points in so that they all meet in the center.

2 Turn the paper over and fold the corners into the center again.

3 Fold the left-hand point into the center, allowing the single flap of paper behind to release so that the shape remains unchanged. Repeat with the top and right-hand points so that the model looks like this.

4 Turn the paper over and fold the bottom point up to the center. Finally fold the side points in to touch the vertical edges.

PLAY TIME!

5 Take the second sheet and cut it into quarters. With the design side down, fold one of the small sheets from corner to corner to make a crease and open out.

6 Fold over the upper edges so that they meet along the center line then turn up the bottom point across the edges of the flaps.

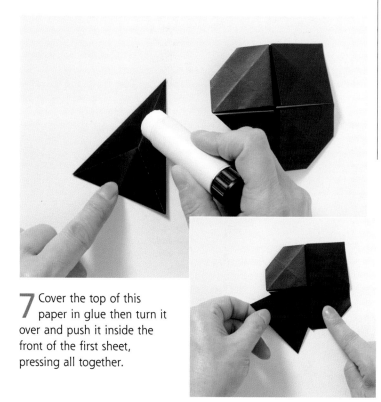

7 Cover the top of this paper in glue then turn it over and push it inside the front of the first sheet, pressing all together.

Clubs

1 To make the club suit follow exactly the same intructions as the spades until step 4. At that point also turn over the top point to touch the horizontal edge then continue as before.

2 Make the second sheet in the same way and fit the two sheets of paper together with glue as before.

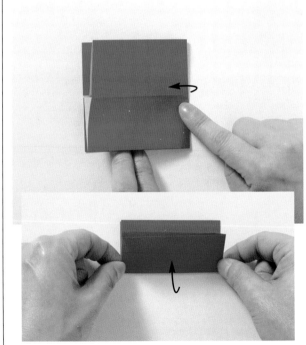

Hearts

1 With the design side down, fold the sheet in half to make a crease then open out and fold the top and bottom edges in to meet along the center line.

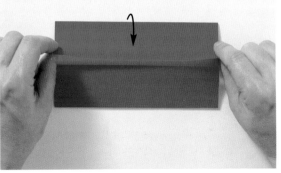

2 Fold the paper in half from side to side then again from bottom to top.

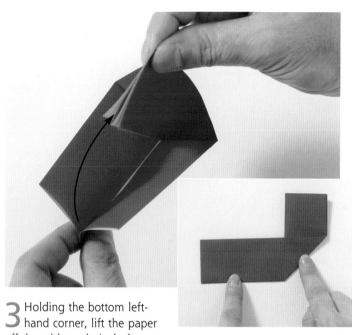

3 Holding the bottom left-hand corner, lift the paper off the table and pinch the two inner flaps, pulling them out and up until they are at right angles to their original position. Put back on the table and press flat.

4 Fold over the upper flap from the right-hand side.

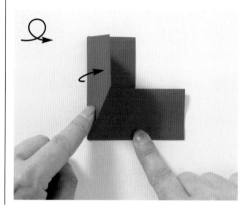

5 Turn the paper over and fold what is now the left-hand edge over to match.

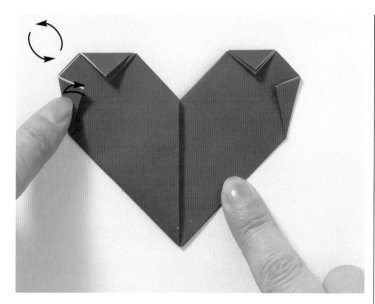

6 Spin the paper through 45° and turn over the corners of the flaps to make creases.

7 Lift the paper off the table and refold the small flaps inside the model, reversing the direction of the creases where necessary.

24 BOAT

Sail away across the sea in this simple origami boat. Go and search out pirates and brigands or have adventures exploring islands and reefs. This double-hulled boat is exceptionally easy to make and will happily float in calm waters.

1 With the design side down, fold the paper from side to side both ways and from corner to corner both ways to make creases, opening out again every time, then turn the paper over and fold the corners into the center to make diagonal creases.

You will need:
One sheet of 6 in (15 cm) square paper

2 Open out the paper and fold the two sides in so that they meet each other along the center line then fold the top and bottom over to meet in the same way.

3 Open up the lower flap on one side and lift the corner of paper from the middle, pulling it out to the side and flattening it into a triangle shape. Repeat on the other side and on both sides of the top flap.

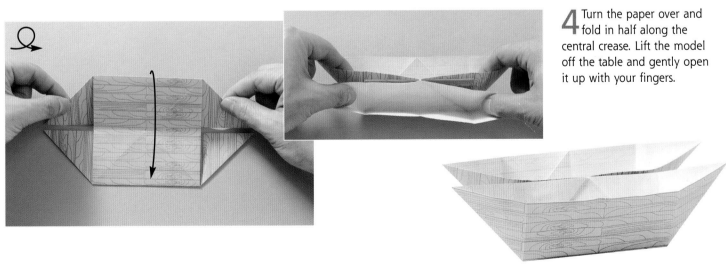

4 Turn the paper over and fold in half along the central crease. Lift the model off the table and gently open it up with your fingers.

25 ROBOT

The robot that can travel through space is the extraordinary creation of science fiction. With this origami model you can create your own much more simply! The model is trickier to make than some but if you follow the instructions carefully he will soon be taking off to explore the universe.

You will need:
Two sheets of 6 in (15 cm) square paper
Paper glue

1 With the design side down fold the paper in half from corner to corner both ways to make creases, opening out each time, then fold the corners into the center.

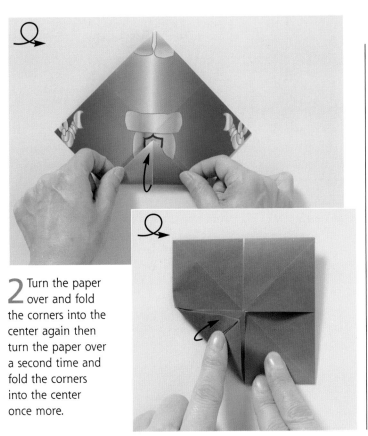

2 Turn the paper over and fold the corners into the center again then turn the paper over a second time and fold the corners into the center once more.

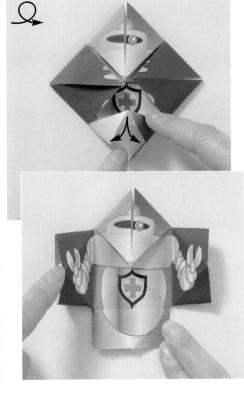

3 Turn the paper over again and open out the bottom flap by pulling down its top point while inserting a finger inside. Fold it flat into a square fold then repeat on both side points.

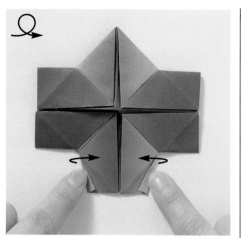

4 Turn the paper over and fold in the two bottom vertical edges at a slight angle.

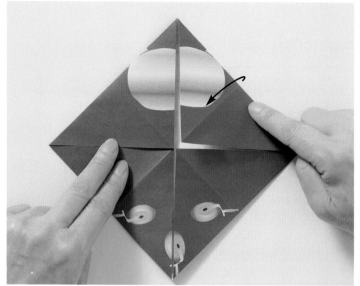

5 Take the second sheet and, with the design side down, fold the paper in half from corner to corner both ways to make creases, opening out each time, then fold the corners into the center.

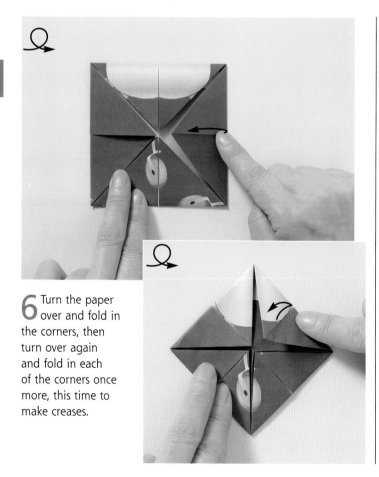

6 Turn the paper over and fold in the corners, then turn over again and fold in each of the corners once more, this time to make creases.

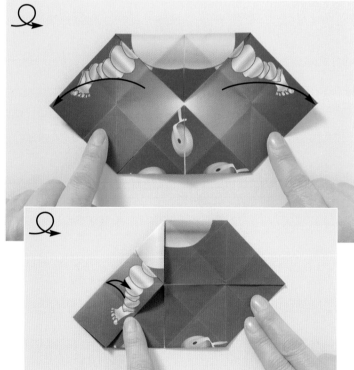

7 Open out the folds just made then turn over the paper and open out the side points. Turn the paper over again and fold over the upper diagonal edges to make creases.

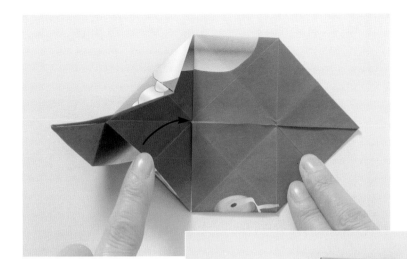

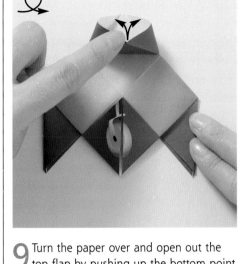

8 Open out the creases just made then push the bottom left-hand point over to the middle of the model ensuring that the bottom edge now runs up the center line and the upper diagonal edge folds forward along the crease just made.

9 Turn the paper over and open out the top flap by pushing up the bottom point and opening out the two halves of the flap, refolding them into a square fold.

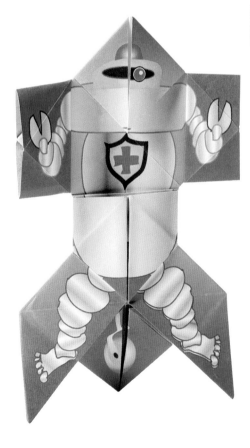

10 Take the first sheet again and cover the bottom with glue then slide it into the top of the second part of the model and press the two firmly together.

26 PLANE

The airplane is the most loved origami model—make one and watch it fly across the sky. This design has wide wings with stabilizers on the end to give it as much lift as possible. Remember that the more evenly you make the model the further and straighter it will fly.

You will need:
One sheet of rectangular paper

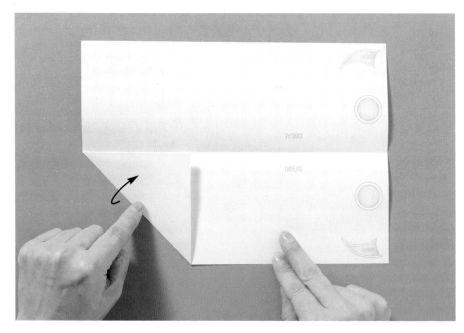

1 With the design side down, fold the sheet in half along its length then open out to make a crease. Fold in the two left-hand corners to meet on the central crease.

2 Fold over the left-hand point, using the lines marked on the sheet as a guide, then fold in the left-hand corners so that they meet on the center line to make diagonal creases.

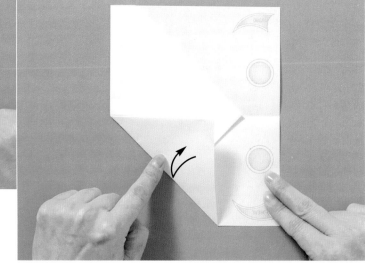

PLAY TIME!

3 Open out the folds just made then turn the lower left-hand corner over to the crease. Next turn the same flap over on itself, using the same crease, before repeating at the top of the model.

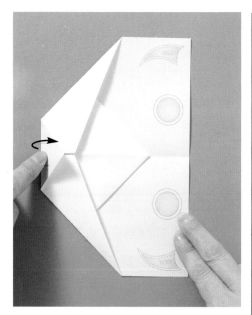

4 Fold over the left-hand tip so that it sits on the point where the diagonal flaps meet.

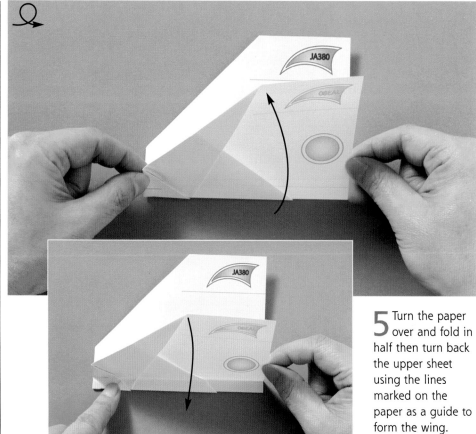

5 Turn the paper over and fold in half then turn back the upper sheet using the lines marked on the paper as a guide to form the wing.

6 Spin the paper through 180° and form the other wing, then press flat against the table.

7 Turn up the edges of the wings, using the lines marked on the paper as a guide.

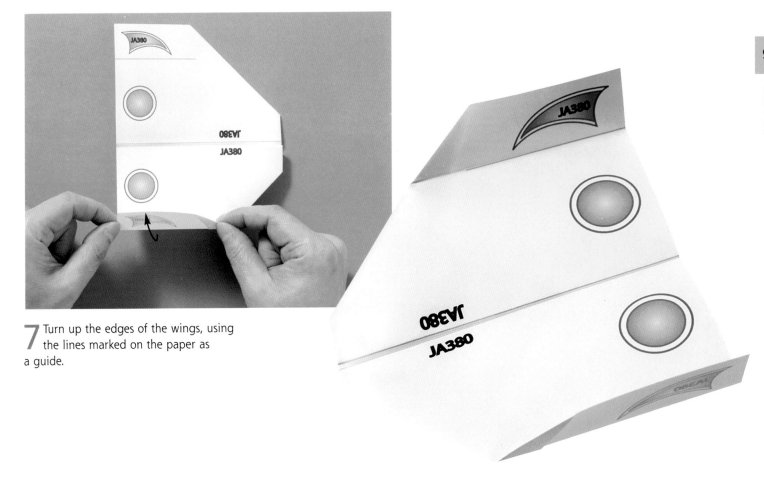

27 WINDMILL

Plant a windmill in the garden and watch it spin in the breeze, or blow into its sails and see how quickly you can make it turn. To make this origami model you will need to use both a knitting needle and scissors so it's a good idea to ask a grown-up for help. Just make sure they don't steal your windmill to play with themselves!

You will need:
Two sheets of 6 in (15 cm) square paper
Paper glue
Knitting needle
Bendy drinking straw
Scissors

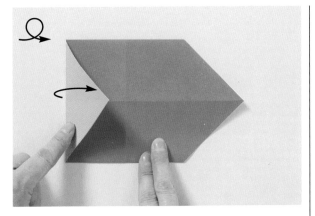

1 Take the two sheets and stick them together by placing a little paper glue in the corners and along the edges. Press together and wait for the glue to dry.

 2 Fold the paper in half from corner to corner both ways to make creases, opening out each time, then fold the top and bottom points in to meet at the center point.

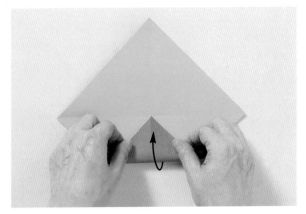

3 Turn the paper over and fold in the side points so that they also meet in the center.

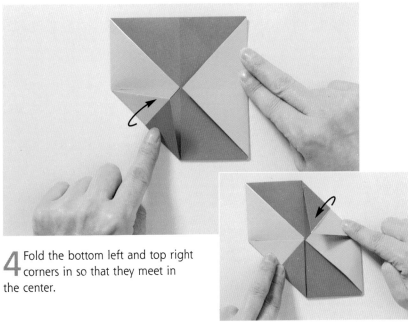

4 Fold the bottom left and top right corners in so that they meet in the center.

5 Turn the paper over and turn in the bottom right and top left corners so that they meet in the center.

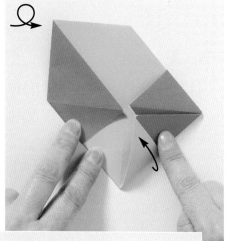

6 Open up the flap on the right-hand side that you just made and pull out the inner sheet from the center, taking it out to the left and downward, flattening it into a triangle. Repeat on the right-hand side by taking the point up and out to the right.

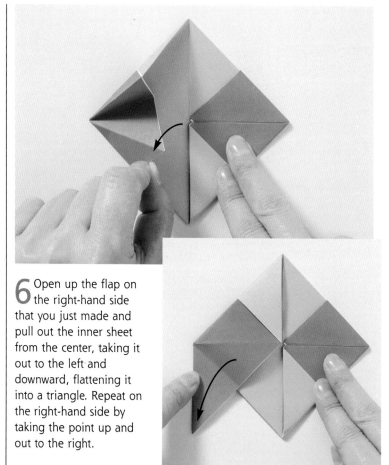

7 Turn the paper over and repeat with the two flaps on that side.

9 Use a knitting needle to pierce a hole through the center of the paper or, alternatively, ask an adult to help you.

8 Glue under the triangular parts of the flaps on both sides to keep the model's shape.

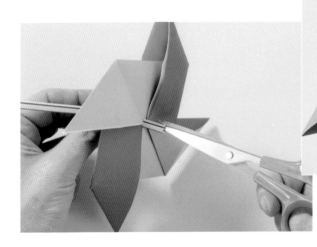

10 Fit the short end of a bendy drinking straw through the hole you've just made then make small sliced cuts through the end. Turn these back to hold the windmill in place.

11 Gently press the flaps of the windmill into shape so that they catch the air when you blow into them.

WINDMILL

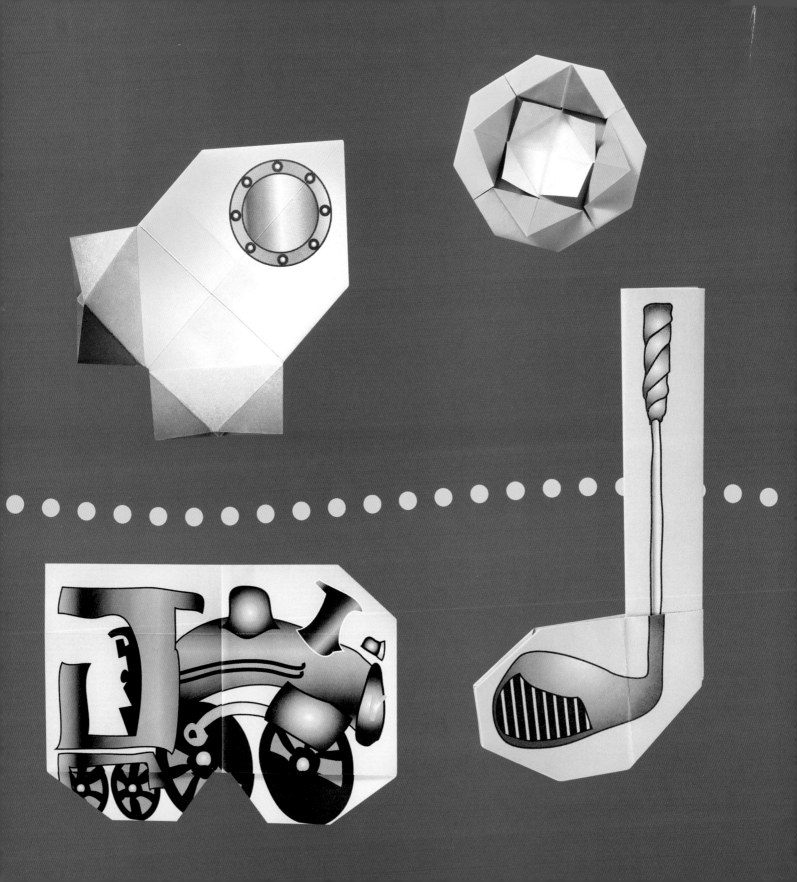

CHAPTER FOUR
Fun and Games

28 SUMO WRESTLER

The huge bulk of the sumo wrestler pacing back and forth, ready to lunge into the ring, is one of the most famous images of Japan. Each one trains for years to become strong and skilled enough to take on any opponent and win the respect of the huge crowds. Your sumo wrestlers might not have the fame and riches of the real ones but they can still face each other across the ring, ready for the contest.

You will need:
One sheet of 6 in (15 cm) square paper

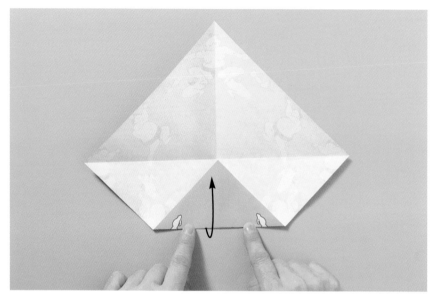

1 With the design side down, fold in half from corner to corner both ways to make creases, opening out each time, then fold the corners into the center.

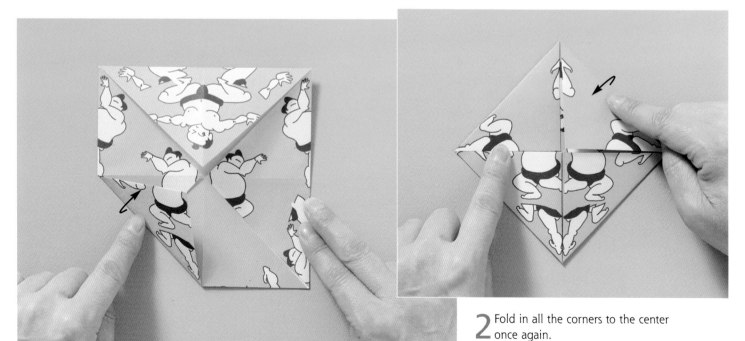

2 Fold in all the corners to the center once again.

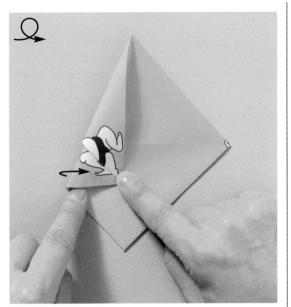

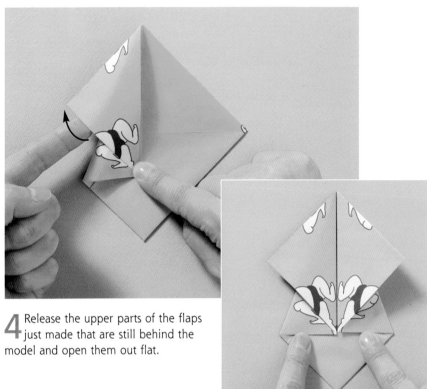

3 Turn the paper over and fold the upper edges in so that they meet along the center line.

4 Release the upper parts of the flaps just made that are still behind the model and open them out flat.

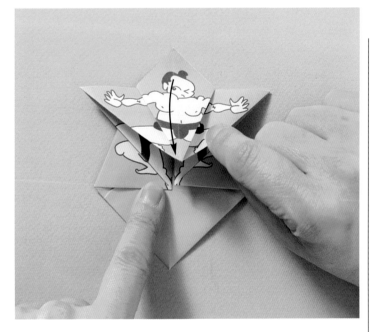

5 Fold down the top point, making a crease line between the outer points, then release the single triangle at the top that is still pressed behind the model.

6 Turn the paper over then fold up the bottom point between the two outer points to make a crease.

7 Fold the left-hand edge of the flap just made over so that it runs along the model's bottom edge to make a crease. Release and repeat on the right-hand edge.

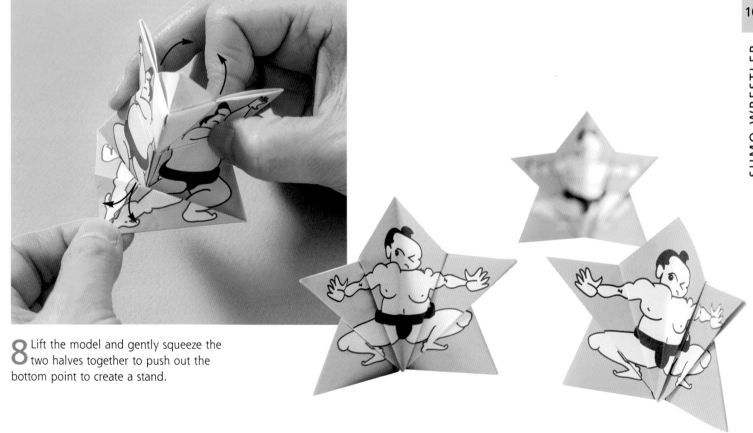

8 Lift the model and gently squeeze the two halves together to push out the bottom point to create a stand.

29 GOLF CLUB

Golf has become one of the most popular games in Japan and this origami design of a golf club allows even the smallest person to take up the game. The model is as easy to make as any in this book—as always just be careful to make sure that all the different angles are correct or you will find it rather difficult to play a good shot.

You will need:
One sheet of 6 in (15 cm) square paper

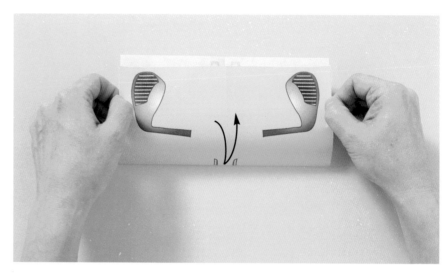

1 With the design side down, fold in half both ways to make creases, opening out each time.

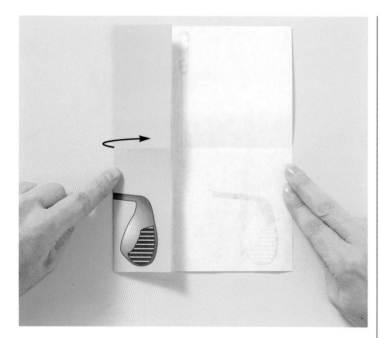

2 Fold the two sides in so that they meet along the central crease.

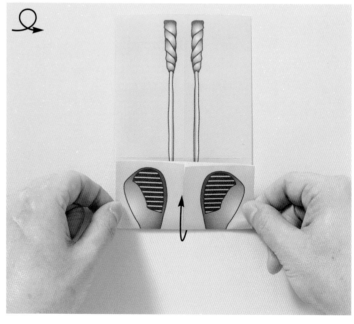

3 Turn the paper over and then fold up the bottom edge so that it runs across the horizontal central crease.

4 Turn the paper back over and fold it in half lengthwise.

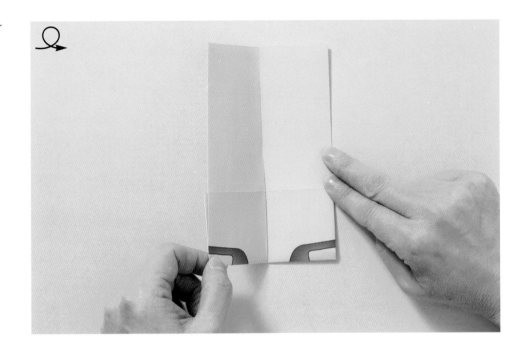

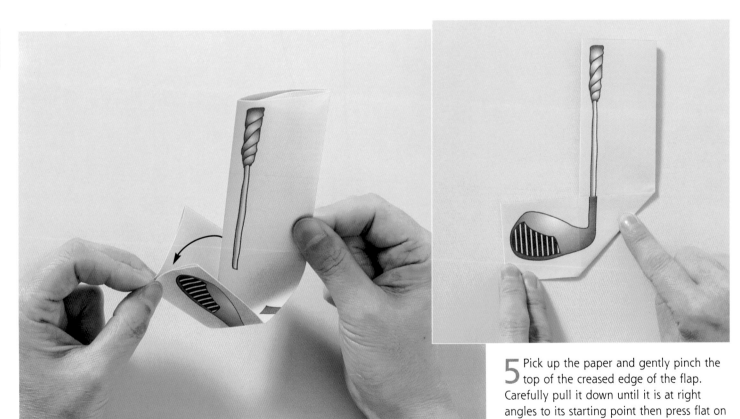

5 Pick up the paper and gently pinch the top of the creased edge of the flap. Carefully pull it down until it is at right angles to its starting point then press flat on the table.

6 Turn the left-hand side of the top flap to the left then fold the edge back over to the central crease before turning the whole flap back to the right to show the handle of the golf club. Turn the paper over and repeat on the other side.

7 Fold over the corners of the base to make a crease then refold the tips so they are inside.

30 MEDAL

Everyone deserves a medal and now you can make your own with this simple origami design. Whether you have won the prize for baking the best cake, running the fastest race, or making the best origami model you can be proud to wear this colorful symbol of success.

Difficulty rating: ● ● ○

You will need:
One sheet of 6 in (15 cm) square paper

1 With the design side down, fold in half both ways to make creases, opening out each time, then fold the corners into the center.

2 Fold the corners into the center again before folding the tips back to the outer edges of the paper on every side.

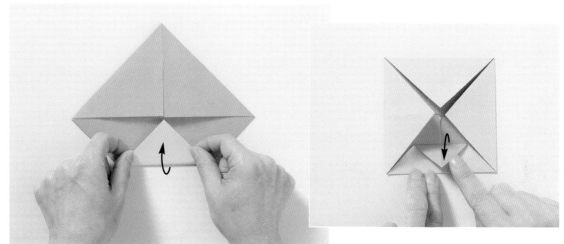

3 Fold back the corners now revealed in the center to run along the creased edges of the flaps.

4 Turn the paper over and fold in the corners half way to the center point.

31 PAPER CRACKER

The paper cracker is an ancient Japanese toy that has been loved by children for generations. The noise is made by the sides of the model opening out before quickly closing with a loud snap. If you want to make more with a different design just be careful to use as thin and light a paper as you can find.

Difficulty rating: ● ● ○

You will need:
One sheet of rectangular paper

1 With the design side down fold the paper in half lengthwise to make a crease.

2 Open out the paper and fold all four corners over to the center crease.

3 Fold the paper in half from left to right.

4 Fold the paper in half again from top to bottom along the center crease made in step 1.

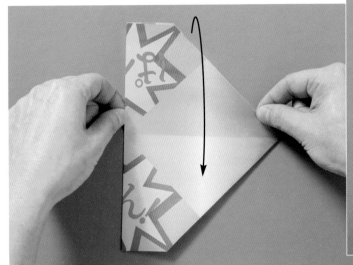

FUN AND GAMES

5 Open the top flap by pushing the top over and flattening into a triangle fold. Check it ends up looking like the image here.

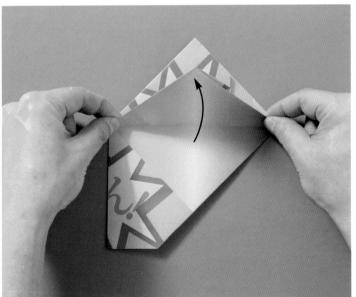

6 Turn the lower part of the triangle fold up and over the central crease.

7 Open out the remaining fold, turning it into a triangle fold as in step 5.

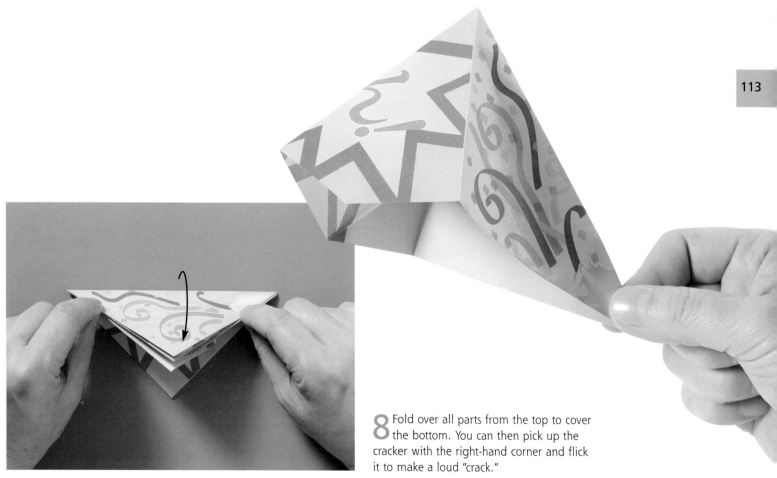

8 Fold over all parts from the top to cover the bottom. You can then pick up the cracker with the right-hand corner and flick it to make a loud "crack."

32 WATCH

Wearing a watch for the first time is an important milestone for any child—being able to tell the time on your own can be a thrilling development. If you haven't quite reached that stage yet why not make this special origami watch so you can prepare for the real thing.

Difficulty rating: ● ● ○

You will need:
One sheet of 6 in (15 cm) square paper
Scissors
Paper glue

FUN AND GAMES

1 Use a pair of scissors to cut out the strap, using the outer line marked on the paper as a guide.

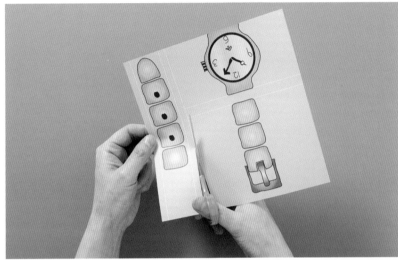

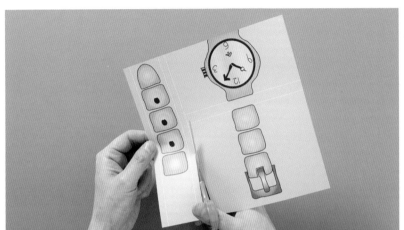

2 With the design side down, fold the remaining piece of paper in half lengthwise to make a crease then open out and fold the two long edges in so that they meet along the central crease.

3 Turn up the bottom of the paper, using the line marked on the paper as a guide, then fold it back into a concertina fold, using the marks on the paper as a guide.

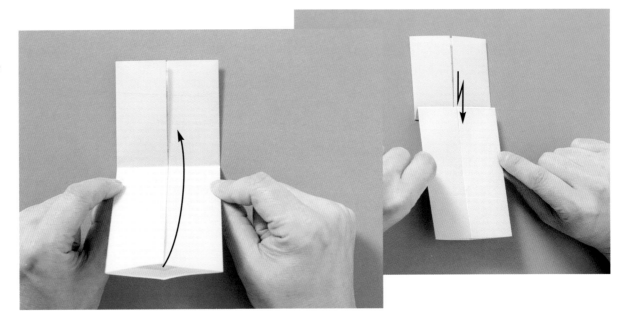

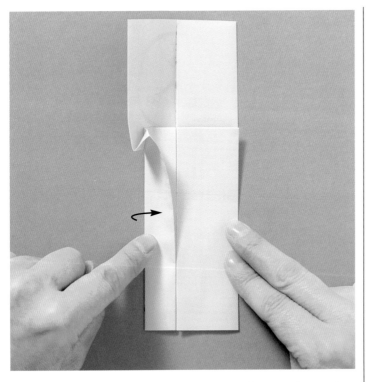

4 Carefully fold over the edges of the longer, lower section so that they meet along the center line, leaving the edges of the shorter section as they are.

5 Gently press down the edges of the folds to create new diagonal edges between the narrow and wide parts of the paper.

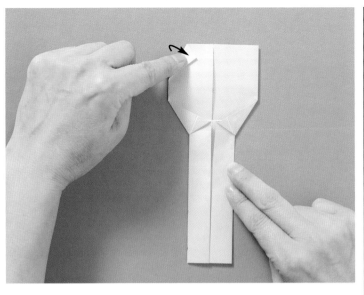

6 Fold back the top corners to make diagonal edges that mirror the creased edges made in the previous step.

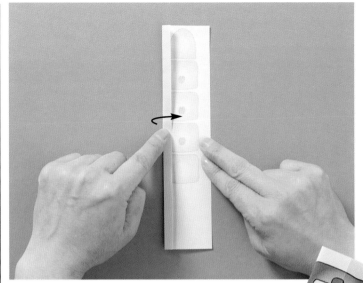

7 Take the narrow piece of paper cut out in step 1 and fold over the long edges using the inner lines marked on the design as a guide.

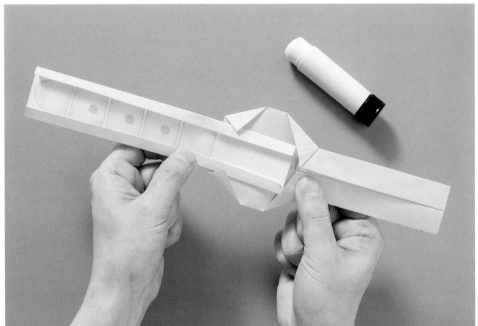

8 Put a dab of glue on one end of the strap and slide it between the last folds made on the main piece of paper then press the two together.

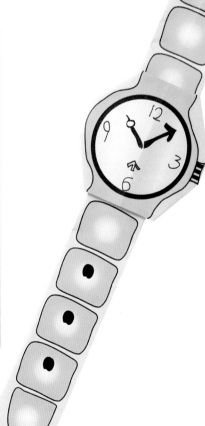

33 SNOWMAN

Winter time can be exciting when the snow starts to fall and the world turns white. This fun origami snowman would look perfect hanging on a Christmas tree as a decoration or standing by himself as a reminder of snowball fights and sledging on a crisp, frosty morning.

Difficulty rating: ● ● ○

You will need:
One sheet of 6 in (15 cm) square paper

1 With the design side down, fold the paper in half from corner to corner through the design to make a crease then open out and fold the upper edges in so that they meet along the central crease.

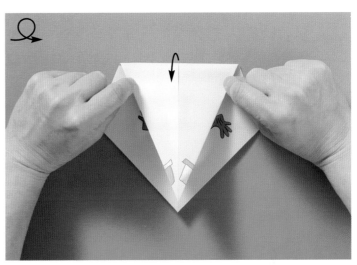

2 Turn the paper over and fold the top point down so that it sits on the bottom point.

3 Turn the paper over again and fold both halves of the top edge over at an angle so that they meet along the central crease. Take the upper flap from the bottom point and fold it over so that it touches the bottom of the two flaps just made.

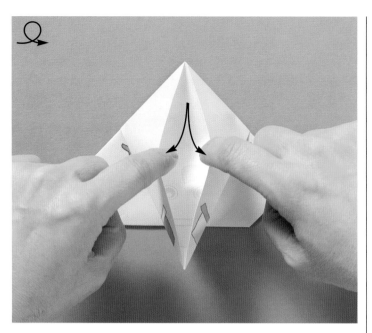

4 Turn the paper over and carefully start to open the long diamond-shaped flap.

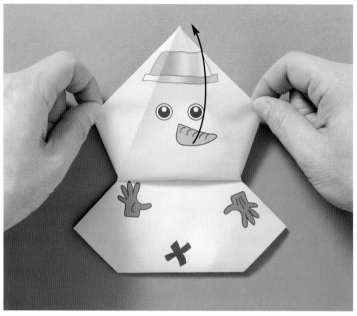

5 As you pull the two sides apart the bottom tip will rise and drop back over the top of the model. Check that the new crease is not at an angle to the main part of the paper.

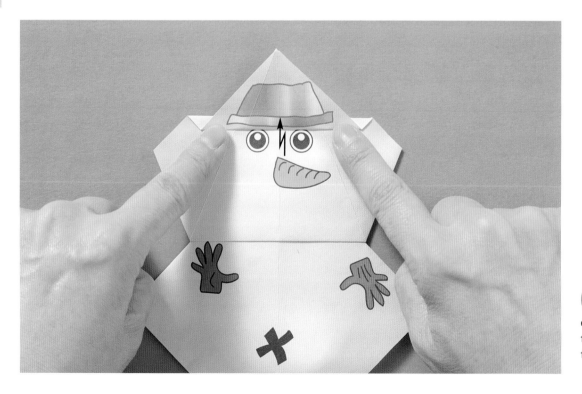

6 Fold down the top tip and create a concertina fold ensuring that the bottom of the hat sits across the top of the eyes.

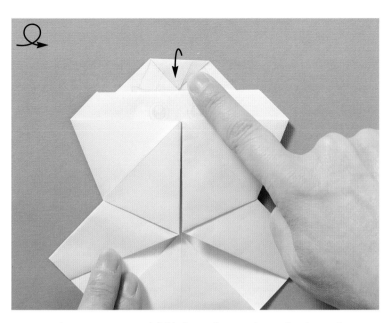

7 Turn the paper over and fold down the top tip so that it touches the horizontal crease.

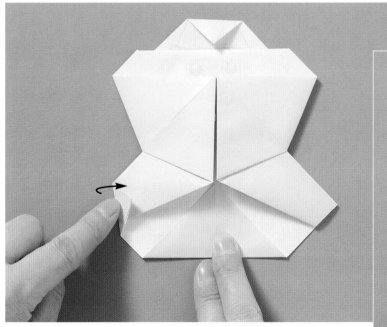

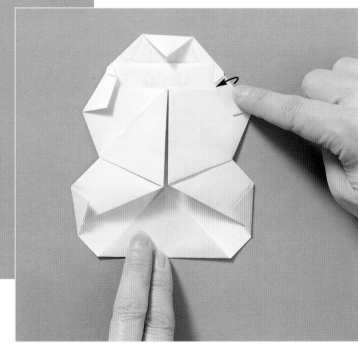

8 Fold in the two outer points at the bottom of the model and the two short edges near the top beneath the concertina fold.

34 STEAM ENGINE

The steam engine is a rare but exciting sight amongst the electric trains of a modern railway. The sounds and smells, as well as the evocative clouds of white steam, remind us of bygone days. This origami model is made with a special fold in the center to give it an extra sense of movement.

Difficulty rating: ● ○ ○

You will need:
One sheet of 6 in (15 cm) square paper

1 With the design side down, fold in half both ways to make creases, opening out each time, then fold the bottom edge up to the central crease. Fold over the top corners of this crease using the lines marked on the design as guides.

2 Fold down the top edge so that it sits along the bottom of the paper.

3 Turn the paper over and fold it in half from right to left, then fold back the top of this new flap to make a concertina fold at the point where the design matches.

4 Turn the paper over and fold in the corners of the inner crease to hold the model in place, then fold over the top left corner.

35 ROCKET

Take off on your final flight of fancy far away into space using this little origami rocket. Imagine traveling across galaxies to planets with strange life forms and unimaginable landscapes. Although simple this little rocket is powerful and strong and will safely transport you on whatever mission you give yourself.

Difficulty rating: ● ○ ○

You will need:
One sheet of 6 in (15 cm) square paper

1 With the design side down, fold in half from corner to corner both ways to make creases, opening out each time, then fold the corners into the center.

2 Fold the top two corners into the center. Turn the paper over and fold the bottom two corners into the center.

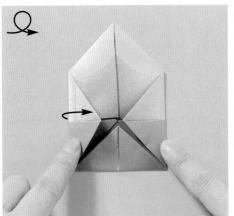

3 Turn the paper over again and fold the bottom point and two side points into the center.

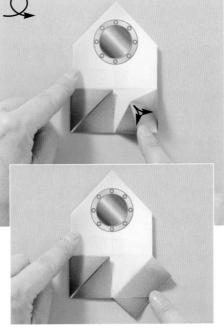

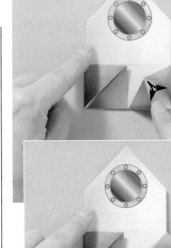

4 Turn the paper over for the last time and gently open out the flaps at the two bottom corners, refolding them into square folds.

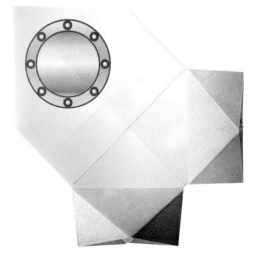

USEFUL INFORMATION

SUPPLIERS

Origami paper is available at most good paper stores or online. Try typing "origami paper" into an internet search engine to find a whole range of stores, selling a wide variety of paper, who will send packages directly to your home address. Alternatively, please visit the author's website: www.happyorigamipaper.com

USA

A.C. MOORE
www.acmoore.com
Stores nationwide
TEL: 1-888-226-6673

Amazon
www.amazon.com

eBay USA
www.ebay.com

HOBBY LOBBY
www.hobbylobby.com
Stores nationwide

JO-ANN FABRIC AND CRAFT STORE
www.joann.com
Stores nationwide
TEL: 1-888-739-4120

MICHAELS STORES
www.michaels.com
Stores nationwide
TEL: 1-800-642-4235

HAKUBUNDO (HONOLULU, HAWAII)
www.hakubundo.com
TEL: 1-808-947-5503
hakubundo@hakubundo.com

UK

HOBBYCRAFT
www.hobbycraft.co.uk
TEL: + 44 (0)330 026 1400

JAPAN CENTRE
www.japancentre.com
19 Shaftesbury Avenue, London W1D 7ED
bookshop@japancentre.com

JP-BOOKS
www.jpbooks.co.uk
24–25 Denman Street, London, W1D 7HU
c/o Mitsukoshi, Dorland House
TEL: + 44 (0)20 7839 4839
info@jpbooks.co.uk

THE JAPANESE SHOP (online only)
www.thejapaneseshop.co.uk
info@thejapaneseshop.co.uk

FRANCE

CULTURE JAPON S.A.S.
www.boutiqueculturejapon.fr
Store located in Maison du la Culture du Japon
101 Bis. Quai Branly 75015, Paris
TEL: + 33 (0)1 45 79 02 00
culturejpt@wanadoo.fr or info@boutiqueculturejapon.fr

BOOKS

The Simple Art of Japanese Papercrafts by Mari Ono (CICO Books)

Origami for Children by Mari Ono and Roshin Ono (CICO Books)

Wild & Wonderful Origami by Mari Ono and Roshin Ono (CICO Books)

Fly, Origami, Fly by Mari Ono and Roshin Ono (CICO Books)

Dinogami by Mari Ono and Hiroaki Takai (CICO Books)

Origami Farm by Mari Ono (CICO Books)

Nihon no Origami Jiten (Dictionary of Japanese Origami), Makoto Yamaguchi (Natsume K.K)

Origami Nandemo Daihyaka, Yuko Tsurumi (U-CAN)

Origami Tegami, Mizutama, (Boutiqye Sha)

Origami Kyoshitsu, Hiroaki Takai (Japanese only)

WEBSITES

Origami Club en.origami-club.com

Nippon Origami Association www.origami-noa.jp

ORIGAMI USA www.origami-usa.org

British Origami Society www.britishorigami.info

ACKNOWLEDGMENTS

The publication of this book could not have been achieved without all the generous help and co-operation give by "my Origami book team," Robin Gurdon and Geoff Dann, and also my husband, Takumasa, and our son Roshin.

Working with Robin and Geoff has always been a pleasure. Throughout the process of making this book, Robin has always put one hundred percent effort into making sure the text is correct, carefully taking notes for all the steps during the photography. Similarly, Geoff always helps ensure that the shoots go smoothly, giving me simple directions that result in great photographs for the readers. The completion of the book would not have been possible if these two members were not involved, and the partnership between author, photographer, and editor is always cherished.

Designing the origami papers takes a long time, as we need to discuss design ideas and work out where the markings should go on the finished papers. This complicated process has always been undertaken by my husband Takumasa and, again, without his help the papers would not stand out as much as they do.

Additional thanks also goes to Cindy Richard and Pete Jorgensen at Cico Books; Terry Benson and Emma Mitchell for taking the style photographs; Jerry Goldie for designing the pages; Rob Merrett for styling this book; and all the others who were involved in this publication.

INDEX